D1223272

COLLECTION OF MASSES OF THE BLESSED VIRGIN MARY

Volume I

SACRAMENTARY

APPROVED FOR USE IN THE
DIOCESES OF THE UNITED STATES OF AMERICA
BY THE NATIONAL CONFERENCE OF CATHOLIC BISHOPS
AND CONFIRMED BY THE APOSTOLIC SEE

Prepared by
International Commission on English in the Liturgy
A Joint Commission of Catholic Bishops' Conferences
Washington, D.C.
and the
Secretariat for the Liturgy
National Conference of Catholic Bishops
Washington, D.C.

The Liturgical Press
Collegeville, Minnesota
1992

Concordat cum originali:

Ronald F. Krisman, Executive Director
Secretariat for the Liturgy
National Conference of Catholic Bishops

Published by authority of the Committee on the Liturgy, National Conference of Catholic Bishops

ACKNOWLEDGMENTS

The English translation of the *Collection of Masses of the Blessed Virgin Mary* © 1987, 1989, International Committee on English in the Liturgy, Inc, (ICEL); excerpts from the English translation of *The Roman Missal* © 1969 ICEL; excerpts from the English translation of *Sacramentary: Additional Presidential Prayers* © 1980, ICEL; excerpts from the English translation of *Documents on the Liturgy, 1963–1979: Conciliar, Papal, and Curial Texts* © 1982, ICEL, 1275 K Street, NW, Suite 1202, Washington, DC 20005-4097. All rights reserved.

Printed in the United States of America.

ISBN 0-8146-2051-5

NATIONAL CONFERENCE OF CATHOLIC BISHOPS
UNITED STATES OF AMERICA

DECREE

In accord with the norms established by decree of the Sacred Congregation of Rites in *Cum, nostra aetate* (27 January 1966), this edition of the *Collection of Masses of the Blessed Virgin Mary* is declared to be the vernacular typical edition of *Collectio Missarum de Beata Maria Virgine* in the dioceses of the United States of America, and is published by authority of the National Conference of Catholic Bishops.

The *Collection of Masses of the Blessed Virgin* Mary was canonically approved for use *ad interim* by the Administrative Committee of the National Conference of Catholic Bishops on 27 September 1989 and was subsequently confirmed by the Apostolic See by decree of the Congregation for Divine Worship on 20 March 1990 (Prot. N. 778/89).

As of 8 September 1992 the *Collection of Masses of the Blessed Virgin Mary* may be published and used in the liturgy. The solemnity of the Immaculate Conception, 8 December 1992, is hereby established as the effective date for the use of the *Collection of Masses of the Blessed Virgin Mary* in the dioceses of the United States of America. From that day forward no other English version may be used.

Given at the General Secretariat of the National Conference of Catholic Bishops, Washington, DC, on 31 May 1992, the feast of the Visitation.

✠ Daniel E. Pilarczyk
Archbishop of Cincinnati
President, National Conference of Catholic Bishops

Robert N. Lynch
General Secretary

CONGREGATION FOR DIVINE WORSHIP AND THE DISCIPLINE OF THE SACRAMENTS

Prot. N. 778/89

DECREE

At the request of His Excellency, the Most Reverend Daniel E. Pilarczyk, Archbishop of Cincinnati and President of the National Conference of Catholic Bishops, in a letter dated November 28, 1989, and by virtue of the faculties granted to this Congregation by the Supreme Pontiff, Pope John Paul II, we gladly approve, that is, confirm *ad interim,* the English text of the book *Collectio Missarum de Beata Maria Virgine* (Green Book), as it appears in the attached copy.

This decree, by which the requested confirmation is granted by the Apostolic See, is to be included in its entirety in the published text. Two copies of the printed text should be sent to this Congregation.

All things to the contrary notwithstanding.

From the Congregation for Divine Worship and the Discipline of the Sacraments, 20 March 1990.

✠ Eduardo Cardinal Martinez
Prefect

✠ Lajos Kada
Titular Archbishop of Tibica
Secretary

CONTENTS

ORDER OF MASS

ORDINARY TIME

Section 1

Section 2

Section 3

FOREWORD

Throughout its history the Church has shown a special love and devotion to Mary. The Council of Ephesus bestowed upon the Blessed Virgin her highest and most significant title, Theotokos—Bearer of God, that is, Mother of God. Century after century Mary has been praised as being "higher than the cherubim and more glorious than the seraphim" because she said yes to God and through her the Word became flesh and lived among us.

As the Church has reflected on the person and life of Mary, it has come to a deeper realization of what it is to follow Christ. In fact, the early Church saw her as the model—the ideal Christian—who faithfully follows the Lord in word and action. The Second Vatican Council referred to her as the Mother of the Church, since her cooperation in God's plan for the salvation of all helped to make the existence of the Church a reality in this world.

Filled with the Holy Spirit, Mary cried out with joy that "From this day all generations will call me blessed: the Almighty has done great things for me, and holy is his Name." Mary's prophecy has become reality as the Church in the East and the West has glorified God for the humble virgin whom God has exalted for her ever-faithful love.

This collection of Masses in honor of the Blessed Virgin Mary is a witness to the many ways and reasons Christians have honored Mary. These Masses are a meditation on the history of our salvation in Christ and the very nature of the Christian life. Through the use of this resource of Scripture, prayer, and praise may we join Mary in proclaiming the greatness of the Lord and ever rejoicing in God our Savior.

✠ Wilton D. Gregory
Auxiliary Bishop of Chicago
Chairman, Committee on the Liturgy
National Conference of Catholic Bishops

CONGREGATION FOR DIVINE WORSHIP

Prot. no. 309/86

DECREE

In celebrating the mystery of Christ, the Church also frequently and with deep reverence honors the Blessed Virgin Mary, because of her close bonds with her Son. She is revered by the Church as the new Eve, who, in view of the death of her Son, received at the moment of her conception a higher form of redemption. She is revered as mother, who through the power of the Holy Spirit gave virginal birth to her Son. She is revered as the disciple of Christ, who treasured in her heart the words of Christ the Master. She is revered as the faithful companion of the Redeemer, who, as God had planned, devoted herself with selfless generosity to her Son's mission.

The Church also sees in the Blessed Virgin a preeminent and unique member, graced with all virtue. The Church lovingly cherishes her and never ceases to ask for her protection, for she is the mother entrusted to us by Christ on the altar of the cross. The Church proclaims Mary as companion and sister in the journey of faith and in the adversities of life. In Mary, enthroned at Christ's side in the kingdom of heaven, the Church joyfully contemplates the image of its own future glory.

The Fathers of the Second Vatican Ecumenical Council thoroughly reviewed the Church's teaching on the place of the Blessed Virgin Mary within the mystery of Christ and his Church, and also issued principles and norms for the reform of the liturgy. As a consequence, the particular Churches as well as a number of religious institutes have composed new Mass propers. These Masses have been created on the basis of the study of ancient liturgical sources and of the writings of the Fathers of the Church of both the East and the West, on an examination of the documents of the Church's magisterium, and on a judicious balancing of the old and the new. As a result of this work of reform, existing Masses of the Blessed Virgin Mary have been accurately revised and corrected and new Masses composed.

Because of the great number of requests from pastors and the faithful and especially from rectors of Marian shrines, it seemed opportune to publish a collection selected from existing Marian Mass formularies, many of which are outstanding for their teaching, piety, and the significance of their texts. The collection was arranged to cover the cycle of the liturgical year, so that this new organ of the liturgy might foster both in communities and in individuals a genuine devotion toward the Mother of the Lord.

By his apostolic authority Pope John Paul II has approved the *Collectio Missarum de beata Maria Virgine* and has ordered its publication.

Therefore, by special mandate of the Pope, this Congregation for Divine Worship publishes the *Collectio Missarum de beata Maria Virgine.* The Latin text may be used as soon as the book appears. After the Holy See has reviewed the vernacular version, its use will be authorized on the date determined by the conference of bishops.

All things to the contrary notwithstanding.

From the office of the Congregation for Divine Worship, 15 August 1986, solemnity of the Assumption of the Blessed Virgin Mary.

✠ Augustin Cardinal Mayer
Prefect

✠ Virgilio Noe
Archbishop of Voncara
Secretary

GENERAL INTRODUCTION

1 In its presentation of Catholic teaching on the veneration due to Mary as the Mother of Christ, the Second Vatican Council in the Dogmatic Constitution on the Church *Lumen gentium* "counsels all the Church's children to foster wholeheartedly the cultus—especially the liturgical cultus—of the Blessed Virgin."[1] In the Constitution on the Liturgy *Sacrosanctum Concilium* the Council explains the focus and intent of the universal Church in its liturgical cultus of the Blessed Virgin: "In celebrating the annual cycle of Christ's mysteries, the Church honors with special love Mary, the Mother of God, who is joined by an inseparable bond to the saving work of her Son. In her the Church holds up and admires the most excellent effect of the redemption and joyfully contemplates, as in a flawless image, that which the Church itself desires and hopes wholly to be."[2]

2 Prompted by the call of the Second Vatican Council and guided by the age-old practice and wisdom of the Church, the Apostolic See has gladly devoted its energies to the right promotion of devotion to the Mother of God. Accordingly, in the Roman liturgy veneration toward the Blessed Virgin Mary is expressed in many wonderful ways, as the General Roman Calendar integrates commemorations of her into the cycle of the liturgical year.[3]

3 Thus on the basis of the arrangement of the Calendar the Roman liturgy frequently in the course of the year provides the faithful with the opportunity of remembrance of the Blessed Virgin's participation in the mystery of salvation. Clear witnesses to Catholic devotion toward Mary are to be found not only in *The Roman Missal (Sacramentary)* and *The Liturgy of the Hours,* but also in other liturgical books that contain special celebrations as commemorations to honor the humble, now glorious Mother of Christ.[4]

I. THE BLESSED VIRGIN MARY IN THE CELEBRATION OF THE MYSTERY OF CHRIST

4 Through its sacred signs the liturgy celebrates the work of salvation that God the Father accomplished through Christ in the Holy Spirit. This salvation is a work that God the Father has carried on through the ages.

[1]No. 67: AAS 57 (1965), p. 65; English tr., ICEL, *Documents on the Liturgy, 1963–1979: Conciliar, Papal, and Curial Texts,* hereafter, DOL (The Liturgical Press, Collegeville, Minn., 1982) 4, no. 161.
[2]Art. 103: AAS 56 (1964), p. 125; DOL 1, no. 103.
[3]See Paul VI, Apostolic Exhortation *Marialis cultus,* no. 2: AAS 66 (1974), p. 117; DOL 467, no. 3900.
[4]See, for example, the Roman Ritual, *Book of Blessings* (English edition, 1987), ch. 29, "Order for the Blessing of an Image of the Blessed Virgin Mary," nos. 1004–1017. See also *Order of Crowning an Image of the Blessed Virgin Mary* (English edition, 1986).

This is the salvation announced by the patriarchs and prophets. "The divine plan for the Old Testament was above all arranged so as to prepare, to proclaim in prophecy (see Luke 22:44; John 5:39; 1 Peter 1:10), and to prefigure through types (see 1 Corinthians 10:11) the coming of Christ, the Redeemer of all, and of his messianic kingdom."[5]

This is the salvation that was fully revealed in Christ Jesus. In the womb of the Virgin of Nazareth, Jesus the Son of God took our human nature and became the Mediator of the Old and the New Covenant. In his paschal mystery he brought about our reconciliation with the Father (see Colossians 1:22; 2 Corinthians 5:18-19) and through the Spirit of adoption given to us (see Romans 8:15-17; Galatians 4:5-6) he joined us closely to himself, so that in spirit and in truth (see John 4:23) we might offer worship acceptable to the Father.

This is the salvation that comes to pass in the "age of the Church" through the proclamation of the Gospel and the celebration of the sacraments (see Matthew 28:18-20), which through the centuries make it possible for all to hold fast to the word of salvation and to enter into the paschal mystery.

This is the salvation that will reach its consummation in Christ's glorious Second Coming (see Matthew 24:30; Acts 1:11), when, having destroyed death, he will subject all things to himself and deliver his kingdom to the Father (see 1 Corinthians 15:24-28).

5 When the Church celebrates the sacred mysteries, it celebrates the entire, integral work of salvation. By celebrating things past the Church in a certain sense brings about their presence and in the "mystical today"[6] accomplishes the salvation of the faithful, who as pilgrims through life are in search of that city which is to come (see Hebrews 13:14).

Mary, who by the plan of God for the sake of Christ and the Church "was intimately involved in the history of salvation,"[7] was actively present in various, wonderful ways in the mysteries of Christ's life.

6 Masses of the Blessed Virgin Mary have their meaning and purpose from her close participation in the history of salvation. Therefore when the Church commemorates the role of the Mother of the Lord in the work of redemption or honors her privileges, it is above all celebrating the events of salvation in which, by God's salvific plan, the Blessed Virgin was involved in view of the mystery of Christ.

Masses of the Blessed Virgin Mary
celebrate the action of God for our salvation

7 Among these events of salvation the Church at the beginning of the liturgical year celebrates the work of God in preparing the Mother of the Redeemer. In her "after the long wait for the fulfillment of the promise, the time at last came to pass and the new divine economy was established."[8] God came with his grace to Mary and from

[5]Vatican Council II, Dogmatic Constitution on Divine Revelation *Dei Verbum,* no. 15: AAS 58 (1966), p. 825; DOL 14, no. 217.

[6]See, for example, *The Liturgy of the Hours,* 25 December, Christmas, Evening Prayer II, antiphon for the Canticle of Mary; 6 January, Epiphany, Evening Prayer II, antiphon for the Canticle of Mary; 2 February, Presentation of the Lord, Evening Prayer II, antiphon for the Canticle of Mary; Ascension, Evening Prayer II, antiphon for the Canticle of Mary.

[7]Vatican Council II, Dogmatic Constitution on the Church *Lumen gentium,* no. 65: AAS 57 (1965), p. 64.

[8]Ibid., no. 55: AAS 57 (1965), p. 60.

the first instant of her conception preserved her from all stain of sin, filled her with the gifts of the Holy Spirit, and continued to shelter her with his love, doing great things for her (see Luke 1:29) for the sake of our salvation.

8 The Church also celebrates God's intervention in human history in the celebration of the incarnation of the Word, the birth of Christ and its revelation to the shepherds and the magi (the first Jewish and the first Gentile converts to the Church, see Luke 2:15-16; Matthew 2:1-12), and in the celebration of other events of Christ's infancy. Mary was intimately involved in all of these saving deeds of God. For this reason many of the Mass formularies, a number of which are of great antiquity and liturgical significance, in celebrating the mysteries of Christ's infancy at the same time honor his Mother's part in them.

9 The Church's liturgical celebration of the public life of our Savior, which was marked by the glorious deeds of the Father, is also a commemoration of the Blessed Virgin, "who shared in the mysteries of Christ."[9] For "in Jesus' public life Mary appears on significant occasions. She was present at its beginning, when at the wedding feast of Cana, moved by compassion, she interceded and brought about the first miracle of Jesus the Messiah (see John 2:1-11). During his preaching mission, Mary welcomed the words in which her Son extolled the kingdom of God as transcending considerations and bonds of flesh and blood and proclaimed that the truly blessed are those who hear the word of God and keep it (see Mark 3:15; Luke 11:27-28), in the way that she herself heard the word of God and faithfully kept it in her heart (see Luke 2:19 and 51)."[10]

10 The Church above all celebrates God's wonderful deeds in Christ's paschal mystery and in this celebration finds Mary intimately joined to her Son. During his passion, "she suffered deeply with her only-begotten Son and, by consenting to his offering himself as victim, she united her maternal heart to the sacrifice of the one to whom she had given birth."[11] God filled her with joy at the resurrection of her Son.[12] After Christ's ascension into heaven, remaining at prayer in the upper room with the apostles and the first disciples, she implored "the gift of the same Holy Spirit who had come upon her at the moment of the annunciation."[13]

The presence of Christ in celebrations of the liturgy

11 After Christ's glorious ascension the work of salvation is carried on above all through celebration of the liturgy, which with good reason may be called the final age in the history of salvation, since in the liturgy Christ is present to the Church in many ways.[14] He is present as the Head of the Mystical Body who presides over the worshiping assembly and whose members are marked as a kingly people. He is present as the teacher who continues to proclaim the message of his Gospel. He is present

[9]Ibid., no. 66: AAS 57 (1965), p. 65; DOL 4, no. 160.
[10]Ibid., no. 58: AAS 57 (1965), p. 61.
[11]Ibid., no. 58: AAS 57 (1965), p. 61.
[12]See *The Liturgy of the Hours,* Common of the Blessed Virgin Mary, Evening Prayer I and II, intercessions, alternate formulary.
[13]Vatican Council II, Dogmatic Constitution on the Church *Lumen gentium,* no. 59: AAS 57 (1965), p. 62.
[14]See Vatican Council II, Constitution on the Liturgy *Sacrosanctum Concilium* (hereafter SC), art. 6–7: AAS 56 (1964), pp. 100–101; DOL 1, nos. 6–7.

as the priest who offers the sacrifice of the New Law and who by his power acts in the sacraments. He is present as the Mediator who without ceasing intercedes for us with the Father (see Hebrews 7:25). He is present as the firstborn brother (see Romans 8:29) who joins his voice to the voices of his countless brothers and sisters.

The faithful who hold fast to the word of faith and "in the Spirit" take part in the celebration of the liturgy meet the Savior and are joined vitally to the event that brings his salvation.

12 Taken up gloriously into heaven and exalted at the side of her Son, the King of kings and Lord of lords (see Revelation 19:16), the Blessed Virgin "did not put aside the saving role given her by God the Father, but by the many ways of her intercession continues to obtain gifts for our eternal salvation."[15] Because of its bonds with Mary, the Church wishes "to live the mystery of Christ"[16] with her and like her and, above all in the liturgy, continually finds that the Blessed Virgin is ever present as the mother of the Church and its advocate.

13 By its very nature the liturgy wonderfully fosters, effects, and expresses not only the communion existing between the particular Churches throughout the world, but also the communion between the Church on earth and the angels and saints in heaven, above all the glorious Mother of God.

Thus in union with the Blessed Virgin[17] and in imitation of her reverent devotion,[18] the Church celebrates the divine mysteries by which "God is perfectly glorified and the participants made holy."[19] The Church joins its voice to Mary's and praises God with her song of thanksgiving.[20] The Church wishes to hear the word of God as she did and to dwell upon it.[21] With Mary it desires to become a sharer in Christ's paschal mystery[22] and to join in his redeeming work.[23] In imitation of Mary at prayer in the upper room with the apostles, the Church ceaselessly implores the gift of the Holy Spirit.[24] The Church invokes her intercession, flies to her protection,[25] prays that she visit the faithful people and fill them with the gifts of grace,[26] and under her watchful and gracious gaze upon its progress, goes confidently forward with her to meet Christ.[27]

[15]Vatican Council II, Dogmatic Constitution on the Church *Lumen gentium,* no. 62: AAS 57 (1965), p. 63.

[16]Paul VI, Apostolic Exhortation *Marialis cultus,* no. 11: AAS 66 (1974), p. 124; DOL 467, no. 3909.

[17]See *The Roman Missal (Sacramentary),* Eucharistic Prayer I, "In union with the whole Church."

[18]See Paul VI, Apostolic Exhortation *Marialis cultus,* nos. 16–20: AAS 66 (1974), pp. 128–132; DOL 467, nos. 3914–3918.

[19]SC, art. 7: AAS 56 (1964), p. 101; DOL 1, no. 7.

[20]See *The Roman Missal (Sacramentary),* 31 May, Visitation, opening prayer; see also Preface II of the Blessed Virgin Mary.

[21]See The Roman Ritual, *Book of Blessings,* ch. 4, "Orders for Blessings that Pertain to Catechesis and to Communal Prayer," intercessions, no. 383.

[22]See *The Roman Missal (Sacramentary),* 15 September, Our Lady of Sorrows, opening prayer; Roman Ritual, *Book of Blessings,* ch. 34, "Order for the Blessing of Stations of the Cross," intercessions, no. 1108.

[23]See *The Roman Missal (Sacramentary),* second *editio typica,* 1975, Votive Mass, Mary, Mother of the Church, prayer over the gifts.

[24]See ibid., preface.

[25]See *Liturgia Horarum,* the Marian antiphon for the end of night prayer *Sub tuum praesidium* (not included in the English translation of the *Liturgia Horarum).*

[26]See *Liturgia Horarum,* 31 May, Visitation, Office of Readings, the hymn *Veni, praecelsa Domina* (not included in the English translation of the *Liturgia Horarum).*

[27]See *The Roman Missal (Sacramentary),* second *editio typica,* 1975, Votive Mass, Mary, Mother of the Church, preface.

The power of Mary's example in celebrations of the liturgy

14 The liturgy, which possesses the wonderful power of bringing to mind the realities and events of the past and of making them present here and now, often presents to the faithful the image of the Virgin of Nazareth, who "dedicated herself totally, as handmaid of the Lord, to the person and the work of her Son, serving the mystery of redemption under him and with him."[28]

Thus the Mother of Christ, especially in liturgical services, shines radiantly as the "exemplar of the virtues"[29] and of faithful cooperation in the work of salvation.

15 In doctrine and language deriving from the Fathers of the Church, the liturgy finds many ways to express the power of the Blessed Virgin as exemplar of the Christian life. Particularly when the liturgy seeks to highlight her sanctity and to present her to the faithful as the devoted handmaid of the Father (see Luke 1:38; 2:48) and the perfect disciple of Christ, the liturgy calls her the *exemplar.* It calls her a *figure* when it seeks to indicate that her manner of life as virgin, spouse, and mother provides a portrait of the life of the Church and shows the path it must take in its journey of faith and its following of Christ. Finally, the liturgy refers to her as *image,* in order to make it clear that in the Blessed Virgin, who is already perfectly fashioned in the likeness of her Son, the Church "joyfully contemplates, as in a flawless image, that which the Church itself desires and hopes wholly to be."[30]

16 In the liturgy, therefore, the Church invites the faithful to imitate the Blessed Virgin, above all for the faith and obedience with which she lovingly embraced the divine plan of salvation. The hymns and euchological texts of the liturgy unfold the beautiful panoply of virtues in the Mother of Christ that the Church, led by the Holy Spirit, has discovered in its prayer and has learned in its contemplation.

17 The powerful example of Mary that shines out in the celebration of the liturgy urges the faithful to become like the Mother, in order that they might be fashioned more completely in the likeness of her Son. Her example also prompts the faithful to celebrate the mysteries of Christ with that same spirit of reverent devotion with which she took part in the birth of her Son, in his epiphanies, and in his death and resurrection. In particular, Mary's example urges the faithful: to treasure the word of God in their hearts and dwell upon it assiduously; to praise God exultantly and thank him joyously; to serve God and neighbor faithfully and offer themselves generously; to pray with perseverance and make their petitions with confidence; to act in all things with mercy and humility; to cherish the law of God and embrace it with love; to love God in everything and above everything else; to be ready to meet Christ when he comes.

18 In the celebration of Masses of the Blessed Virgin priests and all others who have pastoral responsibilities are to strive above all to teach the faithful that the eucharistic sacrifice is the memorial of the death and resurrection of Christ and to move them to take part in it actively and fully. But priests and others are not to fail to point out the power of Mary's example that can do so much for the sanctification of the faithful.

[28]Vatican Council II, Dogmatic Constitution on the Church *Lumen gentium,* no. 56: AAS 57 (1965), p. 60.
[29]Ibid., no. 65: AAS 57 (1965), p. 64.
[30]SC, art. 103: AAS 56 (1964), p. 125; DOL 1, no. 103. See also *The Roman Missal (Sacramentary),* 15 August, Assumption, preface.

II. NATURE OF THE *COLLECTION OF MASSES*

19 The *Collection of Masses of the Blessed Virgin Mary,* approved by Pope John Paul II and promulgated by the Congregation for Divine Worship, has a specific purpose with regard to the cultus of the Blessed Virgin Mary. The *Collection* seeks to promote celebrations that are marked by sound doctrine, the rich variety of their themes, and their rightful commemoration of the saving deeds that the Lord God has accomplished in the Blessed Virgin in view of the mystery of Christ and the Church.

20 The *Collection of Masses* is made up principally of the texts for Marian Masses that are found in the propers of the particular Churches or of religious institutes or in *The Roman Missal (Sacramentary).*

21 The *Collection of Masses* is intended for:

Marian shrines where Masses of the Blessed Virgin Mary are celebrated frequently, in accord with the provisions to be indicated in nos. 29–33;

ecclesial communities that on the Saturdays in Ordinary Time desire to celebrate a Mass of the Blessed Virgin, in accord with the provision to be indicated in no. 34.

As will be pointed out in no. 37, use of the *Collection of Masses* is permitted on days on which, according to the General Instruction of the Roman Missal, the priest is free to choose which Mass he will celebrate.[31]

22 Promulgation of the *Collection of Masses of the Blessed Virgin Mary* introduces no change in the General Roman Calendar, issued 21 March 1969, in *The Roman Missal (Sacramentary),* second *editio typica,* issued 27 March 1975, in the *Lectionary for Mass,* second *editio typica,* issued 21 January 1981, or in the system of rubrics currently in force.

III. STRUCTURE OF THE *COLLECTION OF MASSES*

23 Within the cycle of a year the Church in an orderly pattern unfolds the whole mystery of Christ. This mystery begins with the eternal plan of predestination, in which Christ, the Word made flesh, stands as principle and head, as end and fulfillment of the human race and of all creation; it extends to his glorious Second Coming, when all things will be brought to completion in him, "that God may be all in all (1 Corinthians 15:28)."[32]

24 Since Mary is so closely linked with the mystery of Christ, the *Collection of Masses of the Blessed Virgin Mary* is arranged in accord with the divisions of the liturgical year. With the mystery celebrated as the primary criterion, therefore, the forty-six formularies in the *Collection of Masses* are distributed over the seasons of the liturgical year: Advent (three formularies), the Christmas season (six formularies), Lent (five formularies), Easter season (four formularies), Ordinary Time (twenty-eight formularies).

The formularies for Ordinary Time are divided into three sections. The first section contains eleven formularies for celebrations of the Mother of God under titles that are derived chiefly from Sacred Scripture or that express Mary's bond with the Church. The second section contains nine formularies to honor the memory of the Blessed Vir-

[31]General Instruction of the Roman Missal, hereafter GIRM, no. 316 c: DOL 208, no. 1706.

[32]See SC, art. 102: AAS 56 (1964), p. 125; DOL 1, no. 102. See also *General Norms for the Liturgical Year and Calendar,* ch. 1, no. 1: DOL 442, no. 3767.

gin Mary under titles that refer to her cooperation in fostering the spiritual life of the faithful. The third section contains eight formularies to celebrate the memory of the Blessed Virgin under titles that suggest her compassionate intercession on behalf of the faithful.

As a result of this arrangement of Masses, the occasions and manner of Mary's cooperation in the work of salvation will be celebrated and in the most appropriate liturgical season; in addition the Blessed Virgin's close connection with the mission of the Church will be clearly expressed.

25 In accord with the practice of the Roman liturgy the *Collection of Masses* is made up of two volumes.

The first contains the euchological texts, the entrance and communion antiphons, and, in an appendix, several formularies for solemn blessings at the end of Mass.

The second volume contains the biblical readings assigned for each Mass, together with the responsorial psalms and the *alleluia* verse or verse before the gospel reading.

26 In Volume 1 a historical, liturgical, and pastoral introduction precedes each formulary, in order to assist the preparation for the eucharistic celebration. Each brief introduction indicates the origin of the memorial or title of the Blessed Virgin, provides, in some cases, the sources of the formulary, and explains its teaching, which is based on biblical and euchological texts.

IV. USE OF THE *COLLECTION OF MASSES*

27 If the *Collection of Masses of the Blessed Virgin Mary* is to achieve the objective intended, it must be used properly everywhere and by all.

Observance of the seasons of the liturgical year

28 For the correct use of the *Collection of Masses* the priest celebrant must respect the seasons of the liturgical year. As a rule, therefore, the Mass formularies are to be used during the liturgical season to which they have been assigned. But for a just reason certain formularies may be used in some other liturgical season. For example:

The Mass, "Our Lady of Nazareth," which is included among the Masses for the Christmas season (no. 8), may rightly be celebrated during Ordinary Time when a group of the faithful wish to commemorate the life led by the Virgin of Nazareth and the power of its example.

The Mass, "The Blessed Virgin Mary, Mother of Reconciliation," which is included among the formularies assigned to the season of Lent (no. 14), may also be properly used during Ordinary Time, when the eucharist is celebrated for the purpose of arousing a spirit of reconciliation and concord.

On the other hand such Masses as the Mass, "The Blessed Virgin Mary and the Epiphany of the Lord" (no. 6), or the Mass, "The Blessed Virgin Mary and the Lord's Resurrection" (no. 15), may not be celebrated outside the seasons to which they have been assigned, because of their specific congruence with these seasons.

A. Use of the "Collection of Masses" in Marian sanctuaries

29 As indicated already in no. 21, the *Collection of Masses of the Blessed Virgin Mary* is intended first of all for use in Marian shrines, in order to foster authentic devotion to the Virgin at these shrines and to suffuse it with the true spirit of the liturgy.

This purpose will be of great advantage for the particular Churches, since their pastoral concerns are to such a great extent sustained and nurtured by the initiatives and programs carried out in shrines dedicated to the Blessed Virgin. As the *Code of Canon Law* directs, "at shrines more abundant means of salvation are to be provided the faithful; the word of God is to be carefully proclaimed; liturgical life is to be appropriately fostered, especially through the celebration of the eucharist and penance; and approved forms of popular piety are to be cultivated."[33]

30 Celebration of the eucharist is the high point and center of all pastoral activity at a shrine. Participation in the eucharistic celebration is the principal intent of large pilgrimages of the faithful to a shrine, or of groups that meet there for study or prayer, or of individuals who go there to implore some special favor of God or for quiet contemplation.

In accord with the individual circumstances of the faithful or groups of the faithful, then, every measure is to be taken to ensure that the liturgy is celebrated in an exemplary way and that in its celebration of the divine mysteries the worshiping community will itself become the faithful image of the Church.[34]

31 Accordingly, it has been the practice of the Congregation for Divine Worship to grant permission to Marian shrines for a more frequent celebration of Masses of the Blessed Virgin Mary.

The following norms are to be observed in the use of the *Collection of Masses of the Blessed Virgin Mary.*

a. As long as the liturgical season is respected, the Masses provided in the *Collection of Masses* may be celebrated on any day except those listed in nos. 1–6 of the Table of Liturgical Days.[35]

[33]*Code of Canon Law,* can. 1234.

[34]See SC, art. 2: AAS 56 (1964), pp. 97–98; DOL 1, no. 2.

[35]In the *General Norms for the Liturgical Year and the Calendar,* no. 59 (DOL 442, no. 3825), Table of Liturgical Days, nos. 1–6 are as follows:

1. Easter triduum of the Lord's passion and resurrection.
2. Christmas, Epiphany, Ascension, and Pentecost.
   Sundays of Advent, Lent, and the Easter season.
   Ash Wednesday.
   Weekdays of Holy Week from Monday to Thursday inclusive.
   Days within the octave of Easter.
3. Solemnities of the Lord, the Blessed Virgin Mary, and saints listed in the General Calendar.
4. Proper solemnities, namely:
   a) Solemnity of the principal patron of the place, that is, the city or state.
   b) Solemnity of the dedication of a particular church and the anniversary.
   c) Solemnity of the title of any particular church.
   d) Solemnity of the title, of the founder, or of the principal patron of a religious order or congregation.
5. Feasts of the Lord in the General Calendar.
6. Sundays of the Christmas season and Sundays in Ordinary Time.

b. The permission stated in paragraph *a* is granted only for the priests who are part of a pilgrimage or for priests who celebrate Mass for the benefit of the members of a pilgramage.

c. During the seasons of Advent, Christmas, Lent, and Easter, the biblical readings are to be those assigned in the Lectionary for Mass for each day of the particular season except in the case of a celebration in the manner of a feast or solemnity.

''Proper Mass'' of a shrine

32 Because of the relevance of the texts of the ''proper Mass'' of a shrine to the title under which the Blessed Virgin is honored there, the priests and faithful on pilgrimage usually wish to celebrate that Mass.

But care must be taken to respect the different liturgical seasons, so that the ''proper Mass'' of a shrine is not the only Mass celebrated there. Rather the Mass formularies are to be intelligently varied, so that the celebration of the eucharist provides the faithful with an overview of the entire history of salvation and of the bonds that have joined Mary to the mystery of Christ and the Church.

33 The following is an indication, by way of example, of circumstances in which the formularies of the *Collection of Masses* may opportunely replace the ''proper Mass'' of a shrine:

a. during the seasons of Advent, Christmas, Lent, and Easter, when the formularies provided in the *Collection of Masses* are so perfectly relevant to the mystery of Christ then being celebrated;

b. during a pilgrimage that is to spend a number of days at a shrine or that is made up of pilgrims who visit the shrine frequently.

B. Use of the ''Collection of Masses'' for a memorial of the Blessed Virgin on Saturday

34 As already mentioned in no. 21, the *Collection of Masses of the Blessed Virgin Mary* is also intended for ecclesial communities that ''on Saturdays in Ordinary Time when there is no obligatory memorial''[36] often celebrate a memorial of the Blessed Virgin and therefore wish to have available a number of Mass formularies.

35 The custom of dedicating Saturday to the Blessed Virgin Mary arose in Carolingian monasteries at the end of the eighth century and soon spread throughout Europe.[37] The custom also was incorporated into liturgical books of the particular Churches and became part of the heritage of the religious orders of evangelical and apostolic life that were founded early in the thirteenth century.

In the liturgical reform following the Council of Trent, the custom of celebrating a memorial of the Blessed Virgin Mary on Saturday was incorporated into the *Missale Romanum.*

The liturgical reform initiated by the Second Vatican Council clarified the meaning of the memorial of the Blessed Virgin on Saturday and gave it new vigor by making possible a more frequent celebration of this memorial, increasing the number of formularies and biblical readings, and revising the euchological texts.

[36]*General Norms for the Liturgical Year and the Calendar,* no. 15: DOL 442, no. 3781.
[37]See Bernold of Constance, *Micrologus de ecclesiasticis observationibus,* ch. 60: PL 151, 1020.

36 A number of ecclesial communities celebrate the memorial of the Blessed Virgin on Saturday as a kind of introduction to the Lord's Day. As they prepare to celebrate the weekly remembrance of the Lord's resurrection, these communities look with great reverence to the Blessed Virgin, who, alone of all his disciples, on that "great Sabbath" when Christ lay in the tomb, kept watch with full faith and hope and awaited his resurrection.[38]

This "ancient and . . . , as it were, humble memorial"[39] of Mary recurring each week is in a certain way a reminder of the unfailing presence of the Blessed Virgin in the life of the Church.

C. Use of the "Collection of Masses" on days when Masses ad libitum may be celebrated

37 On days when, according to the General Instruction of the Roman Missal, the choice of Masses is left open,[40] a priest celebrating Mass, whether with or without a congregation, has the option of using one of the formularies in the *Collection of Masses.* But "the first concern of a priest celebrating with a congregation is the spiritual benefit of the faithful and he will be careful not to impose his personal preference on them. Above all he will make sure not to omit too often or needlessly the readings assigned for each day in the weekday Lectionary; the Church's desire is to provide the faithful with a richer share at the table of the Lord's word."[41]

Priests and faithful should keep in mind that genuine Marian devotion does not demand the multiplication of Masses of the Blessed Virgin, but that in their celebration everything—readings, songs, homily, general intercessions, the offering of the sacrifice—be done with propriety, care, and a vital liturgical spirit.

V. THE WORD OF GOD IN THE FORMULARIES OF THE *COLLECTION OF MASSES*

38 The particular objective of every liturgical memorial is expressed and defined through both its euchological texts and its biblical readings. It is therefore clear why even from the earliest times the greatest care has been taken in the choosing of passages of Scripture. It is also clear why each formulary in the *Collection of Masses* has been assigned its own plan of readings for the celebration of the word of God.

39 The biblical readings of the *Collection of Masses of the Blessed Virgin Mary* constitute a rich and varied corpus that in the course of the centuries has been created by the ecclesial communities of both the past and the present.

[36]*General Norms for the Liturgical Year and the Calendar,* no. 15: DOL 442, no. 3781.
[37]See Bernold of Constance, Micrologus de ecclesiasticis observationibus, ch. 60: PL 151, 1020.
[38]See Humbert of Romans, *De vita regulari,* ch. 24, "Why Saturday is the day assigned to the Blessed Virgin": vol. 2 (A. Befani, Rome, 1889), pp. 72–73.
[39]Paul VI, Apostolic Exhortation *Marialis cultus* no. 9: AAS 66 (1974), p. 122; DOL 467, no. 3907
[40]GIRM, no. 316 c: DOL 208, no. 1706.
[41]*Lectionary for Mass* (2nd *editio typica,* 1981), General Introduction, no. 83;* see also GIRM 316 c: DOL 208, no. 1706. SC, art. 51: AAS 56 (1964), p. 114; DOL 1, no. 51.
*The reference is to the 1981 edition.

Within this biblical corpus it is possible to distinguish three types of readings:

a. readings from both the Old and the New Testament that relate to the life or mission of the Blessed Virgin or that contain prophecies about her;

b. readings from the Old Testament that from antiquity have been applied to Mary. The Fathers of the Church have always regarded the Sacred Scriptures of both the Old and the New Covenant as a single corpus that is permeated by the mystery of Christ. Accordingly certain events, figures, or symbols of the Old Testament foretell or suggest in a wonderful manner the life and mission of the Blessed Virgin Mary, the glorious daughter of Zion and mother of Christ;

c. readings of the New Testament that, while not referring to the Blessed Virgin, still are assigned to the celebration of her memorial in order to make clear that all the virtues extolled in the Gospel—faith, charity, hope, humility, mercy, purity of heart—flourished in Mary, the first and most perfect of Christ's disciples.

40 The following points are to be noted with regard to the readings assigned to each formulary in the *Collection of Masses.*

a. Only two readings are provided; the first is from the Old Testament, from an apostle (that is, from the epistles or from Revelation) or, in the Easter season, from Acts or Revelation; the second reading is from one of the gospels.

b. But in special, more solemn celebrations when the priest and the faithful wish to have three readings proclaimed at Mass, the additional reading is taken from the texts provided in the *Lectionary for Mass,* the Common of the Blessed Virgin Mary, or from the texts contained in the appendix of the lectionary for the *Collection of Masses.* The provisions of the *Lectionary for Mass,* General Introduction, section 3, nos. 78–81 ("Principles to Be Followed in the Use of the Order of Readings"),* are to be observed.

c. The readings that are indicated in the *Collection of Masses* for each Mass formulary will be most appropriate for the celebration of some special memorial of the Blessed Virgin. Still, celebrants have the option of replacing these readings with other appropriate readings, taken at will from those contained in the *Lectionary for Mass,* Common of the Blessed Virgin Mary, or in the appendix of the lectionary for the *Collection of Masses.*[42]

41 The following are to be observed with regard to the liturgy of the word.

a. During the seasons of Advent, Christmas, Lent, and Easter (except for the concession in no. 31 c), the readings are to be those assigned in the seasonal *Lectionary for Mass* for each day of these seasons, lest the "continuous reading" of Scripture be interrupted or readings that express the particular character of a season be neglected.

b. During Ordinary Time it is up to the priest celebrant "in consultation with the ministers and others who have a function in the celebration, including the faithful,"[43] to decide which is more beneficial: to take the readings from the *Collection of Masses* or to take them from the seasonal *Lectionary for Mass.*

[42]See *Lectionary for Mass* (2nd *editio typica,* 1981), Common of the Blessed Virgin Mary, nos. 707–712; see also vol. 2 of the *Collection of Masses,* Appendix, nos. 1–21.

[43]GIRM, no. 313: DOL 208, no. 1703. See *Lectionary for Mass* (2nd *editio typica,* 1981), General Introduction, no. 78.

VI. ADAPTATIONS

42 It belongs to the conference of bishops to see to the vernacular translation of the *Collection of Masses,* in accord with the existing norms provided for such translations,[44] so as to ensure that the translation is consonant with the idiom of the various languages and the genius of the various cultures. Whenever opportune, melodies suitable for singing should be added to the translation.

43 It also belongs to the conference of bishops to include as an appendix to the vernacular edition previously approved formularies for Masses of the Blessed Virgin Mary under titles by which she is venerated by the faithful of an entire nation or region or of a large section of the nation or region.

[44]See Consilium for the Carrying out of the Constitution on the Liturgy, Instruction on the translation of liturgical texts for celebrations with a congregation, 25 January 1969: *Notitiae* 5 (1969), pp. 3–12; DOL 123, nos. 838–880. Congregation for the Sacraments and Divine Worship, Circular Letter to presidents of the conferences of bishops, on the use of the vernacular in the liturgy, 5 June 1976: *Notitiae* 12 (1976), pp. 300–302; DOL 133, nos. 911–917.

SIGLA

Documents of Vatican II and Papal Documents

LG Dogmatic Constitution on the Church *Lumen gentium*

MC Apostolic Exhortation Marialis Cultus, on rightly grounding and increasing Marian devotion

SC Constitution on the Liturgy *Sacrosanctum Concilium*

Bibliographical Abbreviations

AAS *Acta Apostolicae Sedis.* Commentarium officiale (Vatican City, 1909–)

CSEL *Corpus scriptorum ecclesiasticorum Latinorum* (Vienna, 1866–)

LH *Liturgia Horarum*

MR *Missale Romanum*

OLM *Ordo Lectionum Missae*

Pa *Sacramentarium Paduense* (The Sacramentary of Padua)

PG *Patrologiae cursus completus: Series graeca,* J. P. Migne, ed., 161 v. (Paris, 1857–66)

PL *Patrologiae cursus completus: Series latina,* J. P. Migne, ed., 222 v. (Paris, 1844–55)

Sch *Sources chrétiennes,* H. de Lubac et al., ed. (Paris, 1941–)

Ve *Sacramentarium Veronense* (The Verona Sacramentary)

Abbreviations for the Identification of Texts

All *Alleluia*

Ant Antiphon

Com Ant Communion Antiphon

Ent Ant Entrance Antiphon

Gos Gospel Reading

Gos Ver Gospel Verse

1 Read First Reading

OP Opening Prayer

PAC Prayer after Communion

POG Prayer over the Gifts

Pref Preface

Resp Responsorial Psalm

ADVENT SEASON

During Advent the Roman liturgy celebrates the two comings of the Lord: the First Coming in lowliness, when in the fullness of time (see Galatians 4:4) the Lord took flesh of the Blessed Virgin Mary and came into the world to save the human race; the Second Coming in glory, when at the end of time the Lord will come "to judge the living and the dead" *(Creed)* and to lead the just into the house of his Father where Mary has preceded them in glory.

1. THE BLESSED VIRGIN MARY, CHOSEN DAUGHTER OF ISRAEL

During Advent the Roman liturgy celebrates the plan of salvation by which the merciful God called the patriarchs, united them to himself in a covenant of love, established the Law through Moses, raised up the prophets, and chose David as the one from whose line the Savior of the world was to be born. The books of the Old Testament, in foretelling the coming of Christ, "gradually bring into clearer light the figure of a woman, the Mother of the Redeemer" (LG, n. 55): she is the Blessed Virgin Mary, whom the Church proclaims as the joy of Israel and the noble daughter of Zion.

Our Lady, who undid the sin of Eve by her sinlessness, "is by nature the daughter of Adam" (Pref); in believing the message of the angel she conceived the Son of God in her virginal womb: "she is by faith the true child of Abraham" (Pref); "she is by descent the branch from the root of Jesse, bearing the flower that is Jesus Christ our Lord" (Pref).

In her sincere obedience to the Law and her wholehearted acceptance of God's will, she is, in the words of the Second Vatican Council, "exalted among the humble and poor of the Lord, who trustingly hope in him for salvation and from him receive it. After the long period of waiting for the fulfillment of the promise, in her at last the fullness of time is reached, and a new order of providence is begun, when the Son of God takes from her a human nature in order to free the human family from sin through the mysteries of his earthly life" (LG, no. 55).

This Mass in honor of our Lady, chosen daughter of Israel, recalls and celebrates this mystery of God's mercy and our salvation.

The first reading appropriately commemorates either God's promise to Abraham ("In you all the nations of the earth will be blessed": 1 Read, Genesis 12:1-7; see Luke 1:55) or God's promise to David through the prophet Nathan ("Your house and your kingdom will be firmly established before my face for ever, and your throne will be unshaken for ever": 1 Read, 2 Samuel 7:1-5, 8b-11, 16; see Luke 1:32-33). The gospel reading proclaims the ancestry of Christ (Gos, Matthew 1:1-17), showing that our Savior is son of David and son of Abraham (see Matthew 1:1).

Entrance Antiphon

Rejoice and be glad with all your heart, daughter of Jerusalem; the Desired of all nations is coming, and the house of the Lord will be filled with glory. *See Zephaniah 3:14; Haggai 2:8*

OPENING PRAYER

A **Lord God,**
you chose the Blessed Virgin Mary,
queen of the humble and the poor,
as mother of the Savior;
grant that, by following her example,
we may offer you the homage of heartfelt faith
and place in you alone our hope of salvation.

We make our prayer through our Lord Jesus Christ,
your Son,
who lives and reigns with you and the Holy Spirit,
one God, for ever and ever.

B **Lord our God,**
to fulfill the promises you made of old
you chose the Blessed Virgin Mary,
the noble daughter of Zion;
grant that we may follow her,
whose humility won your favor
and whose obedience brought us your blessing.

We make our prayer through our Lord Jesus Christ,
your Son,
who lives and reigns with you and the Holy Spirit,
one God, for ever and ever.

PRAYER OVER THE GIFTS

**Lord,
accept these gifts
and by your power change them
into the sacrament of salvation
in which the sacrifices of the Old Law
are fulfilled in the offering of the true Lamb,
Jesus Christ, your Son,
who was born so wonderfully of the Virgin Mary.**

We ask this through Christ our Lord.

PREFACE **P 1** (Page 112)

Communion Antiphon

Rejoice and be glad, O joy of Israel! Through the angel you received the world's joy! Rejoice and be glad, for you brought to birth for us the Bread of Life!

PRAYER AFTER COMMUNION

**Refreshed, Lord God, by this life-giving sacrament,
we call out to you and pray
that as we see in Christ, born of the Virgin,
the promise to Israel fulfilled,
so in his Second Coming we may attain
the joyful fulfillment of all our hope.**

We ask this through Christ our Lord.

2. THE BLESSED VIRGIN MARY AND THE ANNUNCIATION OF THE LORD

During Advent the liturgy reminds us every day of the message of Gabriel to our Lady: ''The angel Gabriel said to Mary in greeting: Hail, full of grace, the Lord is with you; blessed are you among women'' (Ant at midday prayer), and prays each day: ''Loving Mother of the Redeemer, . . . you who received Gabriel's joyful greeting: have pity on us poor sinners'' (Final Ant).

The consent of our Lady, which in God's good pleasure preceded the incarnation (see LG, no. 56), is of the greatest importance in the story of salvation, for the incarnation of the Word is the restoration of human nature.

The Roman liturgy recalls this sacrament of our salvation, not only on the solemnity of 25 March but also, as the Nativity of the Lord approaches, on 20 December and particularly on the Fourth Sunday of Advent in Year B; the celebration of this mystery fits in admirably with the character and nature of the Advent season.

For this reason the Mass of the Blessed Virgin Mary and the Annunciation of the Lord is very suitably used whenever, for a good reason, during Advent a memorial of the Mother of the Lord is to be celebrated.

In such celebrations the Mass readings are taken from the prophecy of the virgin who is to give birth (''See, a virgin will conceive and bear a son'': 1 Read, Isaiah 7:10-14; 8:10c) and the message of Gabriel to the Virgin of Nazareth: (''See, you will conceive in your womb and bear a son'': Gos, Luke 1:26-38).

This Mass was formerly celebrated on the ember days of Advent. Because of its beauty it was frequently known in the Middle Ages as ''the Golden Mass.''

The formulary is to be found in *The Roman Missal (Sacramentary)*, in the Common of the Blessed Virgin Mary during Advent (MR, pp. 673–674), except for the preface, which is taken from the Mass of the solemnity of the Annunciation of the Lord on 25 March.

Entrance Antiphon

A **Let the clouds rain down the Just One, and the earth bring forth the Savior.**
See Isaiah 45:8

B **The angel said to Mary: You have won God's favor. You will conceive and bear a son, and he will be called Son of the Most High.**
Luke 1:30-32

OPENING PRAYER

O God,
you chose that at the message of an angel
your Word should take flesh
in the womb of the Blessed Virgin Mary.
Grant that we who believe that she is the Mother of God
may receive the help of her prayers.

We ask this through our Lord Jesus Christ, your Son,
who lives and reigns with you and the Holy Spirit,
one God, for ever and ever.

PRAYER OVER THE GIFTS

Lord,
may the power of the Spirit,
which came upon Mary and made her womb fruitful,
sanctify the gifts we have placed on this altar.

We ask this through Christ our Lord.

PREFACE **P 2** (Page 113)

Communion Antiphon

The virgin is with child and shall bear a son, and she will call him Emmanuel. *Isaiah 7:14*

PRAYER AFTER COMMUNION

Lord our God,
may the sacraments we receive
show us your forgiveness and love,
that we who honor the mother of your Son
may be saved by his incarnation,
for he is Lord for ever and ever.

3. THE VISITATION OF THE BLESSED VIRGIN MARY

On more than one occasion the Roman liturgy celebrates the grace-filled mystery in the unfolding of salvation when the Virgin Mary, overshadowed by the Holy Spirit and bearing the Word of God, visits Elizabeth: on the feast itself (31 May), before the solemnity of the Birth of John the Baptist (24 June); during Advent, because of its close connection with the solemnity of Christmas, on 21 December; and in particular on the Fourth Sunday of Advent of Year C.

The Mass of the Visitation of the Blessed Virgin Mary is appropriate during Advent when a memorial of the Mother of the Lord is to be celebrated for a reasonable cause.

Our Lady in visiting her kinswoman Elizabeth is an image of the mystery of salvation, in which God ''has come to his people and set them free'' (Ent Ant, Luke 1:68). Mary is also the model for the Church, which God nourishes with his gifts and on which he pours out his Holy Spirit (see PAC) as it brings the message of joy to the whole world so that all peoples may ''acknowledge Christ as their Savior'' (PAC).

In this Mass our Lady is honored as:

—*the new daughter of Zion,* who in her womb (''in your midst'') bears the Lord, the King of Israel (1 Read, Zephaniah 3:14-18a);
—*the new ark of the covenant,* who, bearing the Word of God, brings ''salvation and joy to the home of Elizabeth'' (OP, see 1 Chronicles 13:14);
—*a new creation,* formed by the Holy Spirit (see POG and LG, no. 56), who is bathed in the dew of heavenly grace (see POG), and bears the fruit of salvation, Jesus Christ;
—*the mother of the Lord,* whom Elizabeth recognizes in words inspired by the Holy Spirit (see Pref) and who gives herself completely to the mystery of redemption.
—*a holy woman,* who, hearing the words of an angel, hastens to play her part in the work of salvation, proclaims God's greatness in her song of praise and thanksgiving (see Gos, Luke 1:39-56); a paragon of loving service (see Pref), she is rightly hailed as blessed ''because she believed in your (God's) promise of salvation'' (Pref, see *All,* Luke 1:45), whose humility is looked upon with favor by God (see Com Ant, Luke 1:48) and will be acclaimed by all generations.

Entrance Antiphon

Blessed be the Lord, the God of Israel; he has come to his people and set them free. He has raised up for us a mighty savior, as his holy prophets promised of old. *Luke 1:68-69a, 70*

OPENING PRAYER

Lord our God,
Savior of the human family,
you brought salvation and joy
to the home of Elizabeth
through the visit of the Blessed Virgin Mary,
the ark of the New Covenant.

We ask that, in obedience
to the inspiration of the Holy Spirit,
we too may bring Christ to others
and proclaim your greatness
by the praise of our lips
and the holiness of our lives.

We ask this through our Lord Jesus Christ, your Son,
who lives and reigns with you and the Holy Spirit,
one God, for ever and ever.

PRAYER OVER THE GIFTS

Lord,
may our gifts be sanctified by the Holy Spirit,
who formed the Blessed Virgin Mary
to be a new creation
and bathed her with the dew of heavenly grace,
so that she might bear the fruit of salvation,
Jesus Christ, your Son,
who lives and reigns for ever and ever.

PREFACE **P 3** (Page 114)

Communion Antiphon

God has looked with favor on his lowly servant. From this day all generations will call me blessed. *Luke 1:48*

PRAYER AFTER COMMUNION

Lord our God,
you have nourished the Church with your sacramental gifts
and poured out on it your Holy Spirit;
may it hasten to bring your message of joy to the whole world,
so that all peoples who receive your saving word
may rejoice in your redeeming love
and acknowledge Christ as their Savior,
who lives and reigns for ever and ever.

CHRISTMAS SEASON

During the Christmas season the Church celebrates the mysteries of the childhood of Christ the Savior and his first manifestations. For this reason this liturgical period, though it ends with the feast of the Baptism of the Lord, nevertheless includes the Mass of the Lord's manifestation at the wedding feast of Cana.

In the divine plan the Blessed Virgin was involved in many wonderful ways in the mysteries of the Savior's childhood and manifestations. By a virginal birth she brought forth the Son, showed him to the shepherds and the magi, presented him in the temple and offered him to the Lord. She took her child into exile in Egypt, searched for him when he was lost, and in the home of Nazareth she and Joseph, her husband, led their holy and busy life with Christ. At the wedding feast of Cana she asked a favor of her Son on behalf of the bride and groom and Jesus "performed the first of his signs and manifested his glory" (John 2:11).

4. HOLY MARY, MOTHER OF GOD

This Mass celebrates the "wonderful and inexpressible mystery" (Pref), by which the Father of mercies sent his Son "from heaven into the womb of the Blessed Virgin" (OP, A; see St. Hippolytus, *Traditio apostolica,* 4: Sch, 11 bis, p. 48) to be "(his) saving Word and our Bread of Life" (OP, A). It also commemorates both the faith and the humility with which our Lady "conceived your only Son and bore (him) in her pure womb" (Pref). The humble Virgin of Nazareth is thus set before us as an example: like her we are to receive the Son of God by "treasuring his words in our hearts and celebrating with deep faith the mysteries of our redemption" (OP, A), to reveal him in the holiness of our lives (see OP, B), "praise him with our lips and be faithful to him in our deeds" (PAC).

The texts of this Mass echo the writings of the Fathers of the Church and ancient liturgical prayers, and in particular:

—the thought of St. Augustine (d. 430) that our Lady "conceived him (Christ) in her heart before she conceived him in her womb" (OP, B; *Sermo* 25, 7: PL 38, 937); Augustine praises her faith and obedience and sets before us her spiritual relationship with her Son;

—the saying of St. Bernard (d. 1153) that though our Lady was pleasing to God because of her virginity, yet it was through her humility that she conceived him (see *In laudibus Virginis Matris,* I, 5: *Opera omnia,* IV, ed. Cistercienses, Rome, 1966, p. 18).

The preface should be noted: it admirably extols the virginal and salvific motherhood of our Lady: "What joy is hers at (God's) twofold gift: she is full of wonder at her virgin-motherhood and full of joy at giving birth to the Redeemer." Experts in liturgy rank this among the oldest prefaces in honor of our Lady: it is found in the Sacramentarium Paduense (Pa, 387).

Entrance Antiphon

A **Virgin Mother of God, he whom the whole world cannot contain enclosed himself as a child within your womb.**

B **Hail, holy Mother: you gave birth to the King who is Lord of heaven and earth for ever.** *Sedulius*

OPENING PRAYER

A **Lord our God,**
you sent your Son from heaven
into the womb of the Blessed Virgin
to be your saving Word and our Bread of Life.

Grant that like Mary we may welcome Christ
by treasuring his words in our hearts
and celebrating with deep faith
the mysteries of our redemption.

We ask this through our Lord Jesus Christ, your Son,
who lives and reigns with you and the Holy Spirit,
one God, for ever and ever.

B **Lord God,**
when your Son came down from heaven
Mary conceived him in her heart
before she conceived him in her womb.

Grant that by holy and just deeds
we may show forth in our lives
the Christ, whom we have received by faith
and who lives and reigns with you and the Holy Spirit,
one God, for ever and ever.

PRAYER OVER THE GIFTS

**Accept, Lord God,
the gifts which your people offer
on this memorial of the Blessed Virgin Mary,
who pleased you by her virginity
and in humility conceived your Son, our Lord,
who lives and reigns for ever and ever.**

PREFACE

P 4 (Page 115)

Communion Antiphon

Blessed is the womb of the Virgin Mary, which bore the Son of the eternal Father.

PRAYER AFTER COMMUNION

**Nourished, Lord God, with food from heaven,
we pray,
that as we have received in this sacrament
your Son, born of the Virgin Mother,
we may praise him with our lips
and be faithful to him in our deeds,
for he lives and reigns for ever and ever.**

5. THE BLESSED VIRGIN MARY, MOTHER OF THE SAVIOR

This Mass of the Blessed Virgin Mary, Mother of the Savior, is found in *The Roman Missal (Sacramentary)* in the Common of the Blessed Virgin Mary, Christmas Season (MR, pp. 674–675). Its texts are both ancient and full of beauty. The preface is taken from the venerable *Sacramentarium Veronense* (Ve 1247).

This Mass, resounding with Christmas joy and light, celebrates:

—above all, the maternal role of our Lady in relation to her Son, acknowledged as the King "whose reign is unending"(Ent Ant), as the Son of God (see OP, Pref, PAC), as the "author of life" (OP, see Acts 3:15), as the "sign and source of our salvation" (Pref), as "a light for all nations" (Pref, see Luke 2:32), as "the Bridegroom" (Pref, see Psalm 19:6), and as the Word made flesh (see Com Ant, see John 1:14);

—the fruitful virginity of our Lady (see OP) and her virgin-motherhood, by means of which God gave to the human race the gift of "eternal salvation" (OP), as well as the marvelous way in which "the joys of motherhood" coexist in her with "a virgin's honor" (Ent Ant); this motherhood is the source of her unique status and dignity, for there is "none like her before, and there shall be none hereafter" (Ent Ant);

—the unceasing intercession of the Virgin Mary for God's people, an intercession rooted in her divine motherhood: we ask to "experience the help of her prayers in our lives, for through her we received the very author of life, (God's) Son" (OP);

—the example of the Mother of the Lord: like her the faithful are to seek "(God) in all things and" do "(God's) will with gladness" (POG).

Entrance Antiphon

Giving birth to the King whose reign is unending, Mary knows the joys of motherhood together with a virgin's honor; none like her before and there shall be none hereafter.

OPENING PRAYER

Lord our God,
you gave the human race eternal salvation
through the motherhood of the Virgin Mary.
Grant that we may experience the help of her prayers
in our lives,
for through her we received the very author of life,
your Son, our Lord Jesus Christ,
who lives and reigns with you and the Holy Spirit,
one God, for ever and ever.

PRAYER OVER THE GIFTS

Lord,
accept our gifts and prayers
and fill our hearts with the light of your Holy Spirit,
that we may follow the example of the Virgin Mary,
seeking you in all things
and doing your will with gladness.

We ask this in the name of Jesus the Lord.

PREFACE **P 5** (Page 116)

Communion Antiphon

The Word of God became flesh, and dwelt among us, full of grace and truth. *John 1:14*

PRAYER AFTER COMMUNION

Refreshed by the body and blood of the incarnate Word,
we pray, Lord God,
that the sacred mystery in which we have shared
on this memorial of the Blessed Virgin Mary
may make us always share in the divinity of her Son,
who lives and reigns for ever and ever.

6. THE BLESSED VIRGIN MARY AND THE EPIPHANY OF THE LORD

During the Christmas season the Church celebrates the mystery of the *revelation* or *manifestation* of the Word made flesh to all nations: first, to the Jews, represented by the humble shepherds, ''the firstfruits of the Church from the people of Israel'' (Pref), then to the Gentiles, represented by the wise men, ''the firstfruits of the Church from the Gentiles'' (Pref).

The following points seem especially noteworthy in this Mass:

—the celebration of *light*, signifying not only the glory of God the Father, which dawned upon Jerusalem (see 1 Read, Isaiah 60:1-6), bathing the shepherds in its glory (see Pref, see Luke 2:9), and in a marvelous way leading the wise men ''by a shining star'' (Pref, see Gos, Matthew 2:2, 9-10) to Christ; but also Jesus Christ, ''the glory of Israel and the light of all nations'' (OP, see Luke 2:32), whom the Father revealed to the world (see OP) and who in turn revealed to the world the glory of the Father (see POG);

—the celebration of the *role of Christ as Savior*. The many ''christological titles'' found in this formulary are of the greatest importance: Christ is the Son of God (see OP, PAC) and Son of the Virgin (see POG, Pref); the ''surpassing greatness of God'' and ''God's power,'' ''the Most High,'' who ''has chosen to be born as a little child'' (Ent Ant); ''the one mediator and the Savior of the world'' (OP), by whose birth we are saved (see PAC), who gave ''his whole life for our salvation'' (POG). So the shepherds ''acknowledged Christ as the Savior'' when they saw the Son of the humble handmaid of the Lord (see Pref), and the wise men, when they found the child with his mother, ''worshiped him as God, proclaimed him as King, and acknowledged him as Redeemer'' (Pref);

—the celebration of *the mystery of the Church*, which is foreshadowed in the holy city, Jerusalem (see 1 Read, Isaiah 60:1-6), and which seems to signify the house where the child is found with his mother (see Gos, Matthew 2:11); the Church is founded on faith in Christ (see OP), and is gathered equally from Israel and the Gentiles (see Pref), since the Father draws ''the families of all peoples to faith in the Gospel'' (Pref);

—the celebration of *the ministry of the Virgin* in the epiphany of the Lord, as several texts make clear: ''The surpassing greatness of God has shone around us, God's power has been revealed through a virgin'' (Ent Ant); ''through the Blessed Virgin Mary you revealed your Son to the world'' (OP); ''through the ministry of the Blessed Virgin you draw the families of all peoples to faith in the Gospel'' (Pref).

Entrance Antiphon

The surpassing greatness of God has shone around us, God's power has been revealed through a virgin; the Most High has chosen to be born as a little child, to show forth majesty and splendor in lowliness of birth.

OPENING PRAYER

Lord our God,
through the Blessed Virgin Mary
you revealed your Son to the world
as the glory of Israel
and the light of all nations;
grant that as we follow his teaching and example
we may strengthen our faith in Christ
and acknowledge him to be the one mediator
and the Savior of the world,
who lives and reigns with you and the Holy Spirit,
one God, for ever and ever.

PRAYER OVER THE GIFTS

Lord God,
through the power of the Holy Spirit
consecrate these gifts,
the offering of joyful hearts,
on this memorial of the Blessed Virgin Mary;
let them become the body and blood of Christ,
who was born of the Virgin Mother
to reveal your glory
and to give his whole life for our salvation,
and now lives and reigns for ever and ever.

PREFACE **P 6** (Page 117)

Communion Antiphon

We have seen his star in the east and have come with gifts to adore the Lord. *See Matthew 2:2*

PRAYER AFTER COMMUNION

Lord our God,
grant that the sacrament we have received
may show us always your loving compassion,
so that we, who celebrate with steadfast love
this memorial of the mother of your Son,
may find salvation through his birth,
for he lives and reigns for ever and ever.

7. THE BLESSED VIRGIN MARY AND THE PRESENTATION OF THE LORD

This Mass commemorates the role of our Lady in the mystery of the presentation of the Lord (see Luke 2:27-35). With due observance of the law, the opportune time for its celebration is on a Saturday or weekday around 2 February.

Our Lady, who is given the title of "virgin daughter of Zion" (Pref) in this mystery of salvation:

—in accordance with the Law of Moses (see Leviticus 12:1-8) submitted to the ritual of purification after childbirth, although as the "purest of virgins" from her "chaste womb" she had "brought forth in purity the Son of the eternal Father" (Ent Ant);
—faithfully carried out the law of the firstborn (see Exodus 13:1-2), redeeming with the offering of the poor (see Luke 2:24; POG) her Son, "the author of the New Law" (OP), "the Redeemer of us all" (POG), "the glory of" the "people Israel and the light of all nations" (Pref; see Luke 2:32), "the Lord, the Savior of the world" (Com Ant);
—as "the handmaid of (God's) plan of salvation" (Pref) saw in her Son "the spotless Lamb, to be sacrificed on the altar of the cross for our salvation" (Pref) and offered him to the Father.

This Mass recalls the prophecy of Simeon, who foretold that the child would be a sign of contradiction and that a sword of sorrow would pierce his mother's heart (see Luke 2:34-35); it celebrates the close association between our Lady and her Son in the work of salvation: "Son and Mother are united in the one undivided love, in the one shared suffering, in the single will to do what pleases you" (Pref).

In fulfilling these roles in the mystery of salvation, our Lady is the exemplar of the Church. So we ask the Father that the virgin Church, "like the Virgin Mary" (PAC), the handmaid of the Lord (see Luke 1:38), may "keep its faith unspotted, grow in hope of heaven, and deepen its heartfelt love for you" (OP), "serve you with undivided heart" (PAC), and, "with the lamp of faith burning brightly, go out with joy to meet the Bridegroom" (PAC; see Matthew 25:1, 4).

Entrance Antiphon

Hail, purest of virgins, from your chaste womb you brought forth in purity the Son of the eternal Father.

OPENING PRAYER

Lord,
grant that the Church, the chaste Bride of Christ,
may keep unbroken the New Covenant of love
and, like your humble handmaid,
who presented to you in the temple
the author of the New Law,
may the Church keep its faith unspotted,
grow in hope of heaven,
and deepen its heartfelt love for you.

We make our prayer through our Lord Jesus Christ,
your Son,
who lives and reigns with you and the Holy Spirit,
one God, for ever and ever.

PRAYER OVER THE GIFTS

Lord,
let our prayers and offerings be acceptable to you
as we present them with joy in our hearts
on this memorial of the Blessed Virgin Mary,
who made the offering of the poor to redeem her Son,
himself the Redeemer of us all,
who lives and reigns for ever and ever.

PREFACE P 7 (Page 118)

Communion Antiphon

The Virgin stands, presenting her Son, born before the daystar; Simeon takes him in his arms and proclaims to all peoples that this is the Lord, the Savior of the world.

PRAYER AFTER COMMUNION

Lord God,
grant that by the power of the sacrament we have received
the virgin Church, like the Virgin Mary,
may serve you with undivided heart,
be attentive to the voice of the Spirit,
and, with the lamp of faith burning brightly,
go out with joy to meet the Bridegroom,
who lives and reigns for ever and ever.

8. OUR LADY OF NAZARETH

The hidden life of our Lord at Nazareth belongs to the mystery of salvation, and is an example of holiness: in the home at Nazareth our Savior, subject to Mary and Joseph (see Luke 2:51), spent the greater part of his life on earth. The Roman liturgy commemorates this mystery of salvation especially on the Sunday within the octave of Christmas, when it celebrates the feast of the Holy Family of Jesus, Mary, and Joseph. Many particular Churches and religious institutes also give liturgical honor to the Mother of God under the title of "Our Lady of Nazareth." This title celebrates in particular the role of our Lady at Nazareth in the service of her Son and his work of salvation.

This Mass, with its two series of readings, celebrates:

—*the mystery of the incarnation of the Word* (see Pref, OP) and his self-emptying: "when the fullness of time had come, God sent his Son, born of a woman, born under the Law" (1 Read, Galatians 4:4-7; see OP); at Nazareth, as a real child, he "grew and was made strong, full of wisdom" (Gos, A, Luke 2:41-52), and "was subject" to his parents (Com Ant, Luke 2:51);

—*the life shared by the mother with her Son:* in the home at Nazareth, "as the first disciple of her Son," our Lady "receives the message of the Gospel, treasures it in her heart, and reflects on it in her mind" (Pref);

—*the virginal relationship between Mary and Joseph,* united "in an unbreakable bond of chaste love" (Pref), sharing a humble life of prayer, silence, and work (see Pref), and partners in joy (see Ent Ant), in sorrow (see Gos, B, Luke 2:41-52), and in the upbringing of Christ (see Com Ant, Luke 2:51);

—*the kingdom of God,* which is already present and active in the Holy Family of Nazareth, and which is built up on earth "silently" (PAC) and among the disciples, whose life is hidden in Christ (see OP, Colossians 3:3).

Entrance Antiphon

Great joy fills a father's heart when his son is righteous. Let your father and mother be glad, let the one who gave you birth rejoice.

Proverbs 23:24a, 25

OPENING PRAYER

All-holy Father,
in the wonder of your wisdom and love
you decreed that your Son should be born of a woman,
and be subject to her guidance;
grant that we may enter more and more
into the mystery of your incarnate Word
and with him lead a hidden life on earth
until, escorted by his Virgin Mother,
we may joyously enter
your home in heaven.

We ask this through our Lord Jesus Christ, your Son,
who lives and reigns with you and the Holy Spirit,
one God, now and for ever.

PRAYER OVER THE GIFTS

Lord,
as we offer these gifts of reconciliation and praise,
we pray that by following the example
of the Virgin of Nazareth
we may present ourselves
as a holy and pleasing sacrifice.

We ask this through Christ our Lord.

PREFACE **P 8** (Page 120)

Communion Antiphon

Jesus went down with them and came to Nazareth, where he was subject to them. *Luke 2:51*

PRAYER AFTER COMMUNION

All-holy Father,
look with kindness on those you have strengthened
with the sacrament from heaven,
so that, through the example
of the Blessed Virgin Mary,
we may work silently
at building up your kingdom on earth
and so enjoy its fulfillment in heaven,
in the company of your Son,
who lives and reigns for ever and ever.

9. OUR LADY OF CANA

In the gospel narrative (John 2:1-12) the ''sign of Cana'' belongs to the mystery of the manifestation of the Lord. The Roman liturgy celebrates it accordingly every year on the solemnity of the Epiphany of the Lord: ''Three mysteries mark this holy day: today the star leads the magi to the infant Christ; today water is changed into wine for the wedding feast; today Christ wills to be baptized by John in the river Jordan to bring us salvation'' (LH, 6 January, Ant for the Canticle of Mary, evening prayer II). Again, the Second Sunday in Ordinary Time, Year C, specifically celebrates this ''beginning of signs.'' In this manifestation of the Lord our Lady played an active part, and so the liturgy remembers her along with her Son in the text: ''Blessed are you, Virgin Mary: through you your Son gave the first of his signs; the Bridegroom prepared the new wine for his Bride; through you the disciples learned to believe in their Master'' (Com Ant).

This Mass, therefore, celebrates together the Lord Jesus, the Church as it develops out of the sign of Cana, and the Blessed Virgin Mary.

First of all, it celebrates *Christ the Lord,* who manifested his glory in this marvelous sign and revealed himself: as the Messiah promised by God (see Pref), as the Master to whom the disciples give their obedience in faith (see Ent Ant, Gos, Com Ant), as the Lord, whose commands are carried out by the servants (see Pref), as the new Moses (see 1 Read, Exodus 19:3-8a) and the author of the new and everlasting Covenant, and as the Bridegroom who for the Church, his Bride, at an hour here foreshadowed will ''shed his blood on the cross'' (Pref), when blood and water, the symbols of redemption, will flow from his pierced side.

This Mass celebrates *the Church,* the community of disciples who faithfully follow Christ (see PAC) and ''do what he commands'' (OP, Pref), provide for the needs of the community and in ''unity of mind and heart'' foreshadow the coming of the kingdom (see PAC); it celebrates the beloved Bride, for whom the Bridegroom provides the wedding feast, his daily gift to his Bride (see Pref).

Finally, this Mass celebrates *the mother of Jesus,* who in the Father's wisdom and love was chosen to ''play her part in the mysteries of our salvation'' (OP). Our Lady, in the role she fulfilled in the mystery of salvation in the days of her life on earth on behalf of the bride and bridegroom and of the disciples, continues to play her part on behalf of the whole Church as she now reigns in glory in heaven. With loving care for the good of the human family she begs her Son to help us in our needs (see Pref); she tells us to do ''what he commands us in the Gospel he has given us'' (OP). What is more, we must hold, in the light of the liturgy, that the mother of Jesus, who was present at the wedding feast of Cana, is present at the eucharistic wedding feast of the Church. So the community of the faithful celebrates the eucharist each day in union above all with the glorious Virgin Mary.

Entrance Antiphon

There was a wedding at Cana of Galilee, and the mother of Jesus was there: Christ revealed his glory, and his disciples believed in him.

See John 2:1, 11

OPENING PRAYER

All-holy Father,
in your divine wisdom and love
you chose that the Blessed Virgin Mary
should play her part
in the mysteries of our salvation;
grant that by heeding the words of Christ's mother
we may do what he commands us
in the Gospel he has given us,
for he lives and reigns with you and the Holy Spirit,
one God, for ever and ever.

PRAYER OVER THE GIFTS

Lord,
with loving hearts
we bring you these gifts;
change them into the body and blood
of Jesus Christ, your Son,
who at the request of his mother
changed water into wine
and by this miraculous sign
foreshadowed the hour
of his death and resurrection.

We ask this through Christ our Lord.

PREFACE **P 9** (Page 122)

Communion Antiphon

Blessed are you, Virgin Mary: through you your Son gave the first of his signs; the Bridegroom prepared the new wine for his Bride; through you the disciples learned to believe in their Master.

PRAYER AFTER COMMUNION

Filled, Lord God, with the sacrificial meal
of the body and blood of Christ,
we ask that, in imitation of the Blessed Virgin Mary,
we may follow Christ faithfully,
provide for the needs of the Church,
and together foreshadow the coming of your kingdom
by our unity of mind and heart.

We ask this through Christ our Lord.

LENTEN SEASON

During Lent the faithful are properly prepared to celebrate Easter by hearing the word of God more fully, by spending time in prayer, by doing penance, by recalling their own baptism, and by following Christ along the way of the cross. On this "Lenten journey" the liturgy presents the Blessed Virgin to the faithful as the model of the disciple who faithfully listens to the word of God and follows the footsteps of Christ to Calvary, there to die with him (see 2 Timothy 2:11). At the end of Lent during the Easter triduum the Blessed Virgin is presented to the faithful as the new Eve or the "new woman" who stands by the tree of life (see John 19:25), as the companion of Christ the "new man," and as the spiritual mother into whose maternal care the Lord entrusts all his followers (see John 19:26).

10. HOLY MARY, DISCIPLE OF THE LORD

Lent is a "journey" for the faithful, during which they "more diligently listen to the word of God and devote themselves to prayer with greater earnestness" (SC, art. 109), and during which they are ready to bear the cross with greater zeal, so that with minds and hearts renewed they may reach a more worthy celebration of the Easter festival. In this way they show themselves true disciples of Christ, hearing his words and seeking to make them their own (see Luke 8:15), following in his footsteps in self-denial (see Matthew 16:24), and striving to stand by his cross in faithful witness (see John 19:26).

Hence, if during Lent for a reasonable cause Mass is celebrated in honor of the Blessed Virgin Mary, the present formulary is suitable. In it the mother of the Lord is presented as one who shows us "the example of a disciple, who is faithful to the words of life" (OP). Our Lady is the one who by a unique gift of God was the mother of Christ, and above all was his "first and most perfect . . . disciple" (MC, no. 35).

This Mass underlines the importance of "the word of God" or "the word of salvation" in the life of Christ's disciples (see OP, PAC). It begs divine wisdom for them (see POG), extols the most holy Law of the Lord and the just judgments of the Lord (Resp, see Psalm 19:8-11), and sets before the eyes of the faithful our Lady keeping the words of the Lord in her heart (see Ent Ant, Gos, Luke 2:41-52), so that they may imitate her example (see PAC).

Among the texts of the Mass pride of place must go to the preface ("His mother, the Virgin Mary in her glory, is rightly called blessed . . . "), for in it we hear the voice of Christ echoing the praise of the woman in the crowd ("Blessed is the womb that bore you and the breasts at which you nursed!") in his reply: "More blessed are those who hear the word of God and keep it!" (Luke 11:27-28). It recalls the explanation by St. Augustine of the gospel passage "Who is my mother?" (Mark 3:33): "Holy Mary clearly carried out the will of the Father, and therefore it is a greater thing for her to be a disciple of Christ than to be his mother. She is more blessed in being a disciple of Christ than in being the mother of Christ" (*Sermo* 25, 7: PL 38, 937).

Entrance Antiphon

How favored are you, Mary! You received the angel's message and became the mother of God's Word. How favored are you, for you kept in your heart those words from heaven and became the disciple of God's Word.

OPENING PRAYER

**Lord our God,
through the Blessed Virgin Mary
you have shown us the example of a disciple,
who is faithful to the words of life;
open our hearts to receive your saving word,
so that by the power of the Holy Spirit
it may speak to us in our daily lives
and bring forth a rich harvest of holiness.**

**Grant this through our Lord Jesus Christ, your Son,
who lives and reigns with you and the Holy Spirit,
one God, for ever and ever.**

PRAYER OVER THE GIFTS

**Lord God,
look with favor on the gifts
we offer with grateful hearts
on this memorial of the Blessed Virgin Mary,
mother and disciple of your Son;
grant that through these gifts we may receive
grace and wisdom in abundance,
for these are beyond our human strength.**

We ask this through Christ our Lord.

PREFACE **P 10** (Page 123)

Communion Antiphon

Blessed are they who hear the word of God and keep it!

Luke 11:28

PRAYER AFTER COMMUNION

Lord God,
filled with the joy that comes from this sacrament,
we ask that by imitating the Blessed Virgin Mary
we may be true disciples of Christ,
eagerly hearing his words
and putting them into practice.

We ask this through Christ our Lord.

11. THE BLESSED VIRGIN MARY AT THE FOOT OF THE CROSS

I

Lent unfolds like the journey of Jesus to the holy city of Jerusalem, the place of his sacrifice: as it progresses, there is more frequent meditation on the mystery of his passion. So too in the hearts of the faithful there is more frequent remembrance of the compassion of our Lady.

In the propers of Masses of particular Churches and of religious institutes there are many formularies in honor of the mother sharing in the passion of her Son. The formulary set out here, with the exception of the preface, comes from the *Proprium missarum Ordinis Fratrum Servorum beatae Mariae Virginis,* Curia Generalis OSM, Rome, 1972, pp. 24–27.

The texts of the Mass reflect on the mystery of Christ's passion, mysteriously filled out through the present sufferings of his members as they face the ''many trials of this life'' (OP). The words of the apostle: ''I fill out in my flesh what is lacking in the sufferings of Christ, for the sake of his Body, which is the Church'' (Com Ant, Colossians 1:24), are appropriately used in this celebration.

Our Lady, ''queen of heaven and earth'' (Gos Ver), stood by the cross of her Son (see Ent Ant, Gos, John 19:25-27), ''in his agony'' (OP), ''mournful'' (Gos Ver), yet full of ''courage'' and ''faith'' (Pref), playing many roles in the mystery of salvation, and fulfilling ''in her person the prophecies of old'' (Pref). In relation to her Son, dying on the cross, our Lady stands out as:

—*the handmaid of the Redeemer* (see POG), the mother sharing his sufferings, united with the sacrifice of her Son, the high priest (see PAC);

—*the new Eve,* fulfilling the prophecy of the saving role of the ''woman'' (see Genesis 3:15; John 19:26; Revelation 12:1): as the first woman shared ''in bringing death,'' so the second woman, Mary, shared ''in restoring life'' (Pref, see LG, no. 56);

—*the mother of Zion,* acclaimed by all peoples as they say: ''All find their home in you'' (Psalm 87:7), for she welcomes with a mother's love all who have been scattered but are now gathered into unity by the death of Christ (Pref, see John 11:52);

—*the image of the Church,* which as it looks on the Virgin ''draws inspiration from her courage and keeps constant faith with its Bridegroom'' (Pref, see LG, no. 64).

Entrance Antiphon

There by the cross of Jesus stood his mother, the sister of his mother, Mary the wife of Cleophas, and Mary Magdalene. *John 19:25*

OPENING PRAYER

**Lord our God,
in your mysterious wisdom
you fill out the passion of Christ
through the suffering that his members endure
in the many trials of this life.**

**As you chose to have the mournful mother
stand by your Son in his agony on the cross,
grant that we too may bring love and comfort
to our brothers and sisters in distress.**

**We ask this through our Lord Jesus Christ, your Son,
who lives and reigns with you and the Holy Spirit,
one God, for ever and ever.**

PRAYER OVER THE GIFTS

**Lord,
graciously receive the offerings of your family
and make them the sacrament of our redemption,
which Mary faithfully served
at the altar of the cross.**

We ask this through Christ our Lord.

PREFACE **P 11** (Page 124)

Communion Antiphon

I fill out in my flesh what is lacking in the sufferings of Christ, for the sake of his Body, which is the Church. *Colossians 1:24*

PRAYER AFTER COMMUNION

Lord God,
we have received the pledge of salvation
and now we offer this prayer.

Grant that the Holy Spirit, the Paraclete,
poured out upon your Church,
may descend in power on all peoples,
whom Christ, the high priest, claims
as the reward of the sacrifice
he offered on the cross
in the presence of his sorrowing mother.

We ask this through Christ our Lord.

12. THE BLESSED VIRGIN MARY AT THE FOOT OF THE CROSS

II

This Mass in celebration of Christ's saving passion also honors the part played by the Blessed Virgin in achieving our salvation. When Mary became the mother of Christ "by the power of the Holy Spirit" (Pref), she became by a further gift of divine love "a partner in his passion" (Pref), a mother suffering with him (OP, A, OP, B).

The beginning of the Mass echoes the prophecy of Simeon, which links the destiny of the Son and the Mother and foretells that Christ would be a sign that would be contested and that the Virgin's soul would be pierced by a sword of sorrow (see Ent Ant, Luke 2:34-35).

The prayers of the Mass recall the plan of salvation, by which God joined the suffering of the mother with the suffering of her Son (OP, A, OP, B), and decreed that "the new Eve should stand by the cross of the new Adam" (Pref).

The co-suffering of the Blessed Virgin in the drama of salvation is rightly celebrated, because she stood by the cross of the Lord (see Gos, John 19:25-27) "firm in faith, strong in hope, burning with love" (Gos Ver); there she did not spare her own life when her nation was brought low (see 1 Read, Judith 13:17-20); she endured the greatest of pains in bringing forth to new and divine life the family of the Church, though she had brought forth her Son without the pains of childbirth (see Pref); hence the faithful glorify her as they say, "How blessed was the Virgin Mary in her sufferings: she gained the palm of living martyrdom at the foot of the cross of her Son" (Com Ant, A).

What took place in reality in the passion of Christ is now celebrated in sacramental signs; and so we pray that "the sacrifice of the altar, offered in union with the Virgin, may wipe away our sins and open for us the gates of heaven" (POG). The faithful, as they share in the sufferings of Christ, are to rejoice, "so that (they) may be filled with joy when he comes in glory" (Com Ant, B, 1 Peter 4:13), and, by carrying their cross each day, they may come to share in the resurrection of Christ (see PAC).

The texts of the Mass come from the *Proprium missarum Ordinis Fratrum Servorum beatae Mariae Virginis*, Curia Generalis OSM, Rome, 1972, pp. 57–60.

Entrance Antiphon

Simeon said to Mary: This child is destined to be a sign which people will reject; he is set for the fall and rising of many in Israel; and your own soul a sword shall pierce. *Luke 2:34-35*

OPENING PRAYER

A **Lord our God,**
you placed at the side of your suffering Son
his mother to suffer with him,
so that the human race,
deceived by the wiles of the devil,
might become a new and resplendent creation.

Grant that your people may put aside their inheritance of sin
and put on the newness of life
won by Christ the Redeemer,
who lives and reigns with you and the Holy Spirit,
one God, for ever and ever.

B **Lord God,**
you decreed that the mother of your Son
should stand by his cross, suffering with him.
Safeguard in your family
the fruits of your great work of redemption
and in your goodness
make them grow daily more and more.

We ask this through our Lord Jesus Christ, your Son,
who lives and reigns with you and the Holy Spirit,
one God, for ever and ever.

PRAYER OVER THE GIFTS

**Lord,
let our gifts be consumed
by the fire of the Holy Spirit,
so that the sacrifice of the altar,
offered in union with the Virgin,
may wipe away our sins
and open for us the gates of heaven.**

We ask this through Christ our Lord.

PREFACE **P 12** (Page 125)

Communion Antiphon

A **How blessed was the Virgin Mary in her sufferings: she gained the palm of living martyrdom at the foot of the cross of her Son.**

B **Rejoice as you share in the sufferings of Christ, so that you may be filled with joy when he comes in glory.** *1 Peter 4:13*

PRAYER AFTER COMMUNION

**Lord God,
protect your servants,
whose hunger and thirst
you have satisfied in this sacrament;
as we call to mind Mary's suffering with Christ,
grant that by carrying our cross each day
we may come to share in his resurrection,
for he lives and reigns for ever and ever.**

13. THE COMMENDING OF THE BLESSED VIRGIN MARY

The words of Jesus, dying on the cross: "Behold your son . . . Behold your mother" (John 19:26-27), are seen by the Church as a special parting gift, by which Christ the Lord "entrusted" to his Virgin Mother "all his disciples as her children" (Leo XIII, Encyclical Letter *Octobri mense:* ASS 24 [1891–1892] p. 195), and entrusted his mother to his disciples to be honored and revered. Hence "a deep bond of love is fashioned between the Blessed Virgin Mary and his faithful disciples" (Pref), which is honored and celebrated in this Mass.

The commending of the disciples: it is primarily God who is glorified, for making "a home for the Blessed Virgin in the Church as the joyful mother of children" (Ent Ant, see Psalm 113:9). Our Lady is called "mother of those who believe" (Pref), to whom the faithful turn with full confidence; Jesus Christ is more than once referred to as the one who "entrusted us to his Virgin Mother as her children" (PAC, see OP, POG, Pref). This act of commending is part of the mystery of Christ's passion and the Virgin's co-suffering; the liturgy therefore refers to the Blessed Virgin as one who "stood by the cross and tenderly looked on the wounds of her Son, whose death she knew would redeem the world" (Gos Ver), and it places on her lips the words of the apostle: "I endure all for the sake of the elect, so that they too may achieve salvation in Christ Jesus with eternal glory" (Com Ant, 2 Timothy 2:10). With Mary in mind the liturgy sets before the faithful the wonderful example of the mother of the Maccabees, who saw her sons dying, yet bore this with courage because of her hope in God (1 Read, 2 Maccabees 7:1, 20-29).

The commending of the Virgin: our Lady also was entrusted by Christ to the loving care of the beloved disciple: "To the virgin John, Christ, dying on the cross, entrusted his Virgin Mother" (LH, 27 December, Ant 2 at morning prayer). In John Christ made all his disciples "living signs of his own love for her" (POG, see Ve 1276): they "receive her as a precious inheritance from their Master" (Pref), and in heeding what she says (see Pref, John 2:5) they conscientiously "keep the words of their Master" (Pref).

Entrance Antiphon

The Lord is enthroned above all nations, God's glory is above the heavens. The Lord makes a home for the Blessed Virgin in the Church as the joyful mother of children. *See Psalm 113:4, 9*

OPENING PRAYER

All-holy Father,
you chose the Easter mystery
as the way of our salvation;
grant that we, whom Jesus entrusted from the cross
to his Virgin Mother,
may be numbered among your adopted children.

We ask this through our Lord Jesus Christ, your Son,
who lives and reigns with you and the Holy Spirit,
one God, for ever and ever.

PRAYER OVER THE GIFTS

Lord,
receive the gifts we joyfully present,
that they may become the body and blood
of our Lord Jesus Christ,
who on the cross entrusted all his followers
in the person of John
to the Virgin Mother as her children,
and entrusted her to them
as living signs of his own love for her,
for he lives and reigns for ever and ever.

PREFACE **P 13** (Page 126)

Communion Antiphon

I endure all for the sake of the elect, so that they too may achieve salvation in Christ Jesus with eternal glory. *2 Timothy 2:10*

PRAYER AFTER COMMUNION

Lord God,
let this sacred table increase our filial love,
for here we are nourished
by the body and blood of Christ,
who when dying on the cross
delivered his spirit into your hands
and entrusted us to his Virgin Mother as her children.

We ask this through Christ our Lord.

14. THE BLESSED VIRGIN MARY, MOTHER OF RECONCILIATION

The season of Lent has both a baptismal and a penitential character (see SC, art. 109). From Ash Wednesday the words of the apostle re-echo in the liturgy: "We beg you on behalf of Christ: be reconciled with God" (2 Corinthians 5:20). This text is also used in this Mass (1 Read, 2 Corinthians 5:17-21).

The Church has with ever greater clarity acknowledged the role of our Lady in reconciling sinners with God. The Fathers of the Church in the early centuries, in discussing the mystery of the incarnation of the Word, speak frequently of the virginal womb of the mother of the Lord as the place where "peace" between God and the human race came to be. The teaching of the popes of our own age fits in admirably with this patristic thought: the Blessed Virgin, in the words of Pope John Paul II, "became associated with God in the very work of reconciliation through her divine maternity" (Postsynodal Apostolic Exhortation *Reconciliatio et paenitentiae,* no. 35: AAS 77 [1985], p. 275).

In the Middle Ages ecclesiastical writers, deepening their understanding of the maternal role of the Blessed Virgin, gave her the titles of "way of reconciliation," "general cause of reconciliation" as well as "mother of reconciliation," because it was from her that Jesus Christ, the "reconciliation of sinners," was born: "There is no reconciliation," says St. Anselm of Canterbury (d. 1109), "except the reconciliation that you bore in purity" (H. Barré, *Prières anciennes de l'Occident à la Mère du Sauveur,* Ed. P. Lethielleux, Paris, 1963, p. 305). Hence the faithful turn to the Blessed Virgin in order that, through her intercession, they may obtain "the grace of reconciliation," and, from the twelfth century at least, devoutly venerate her under the title of "refuge of sinners."

In our own day the Blessed Virgin is honored liturgically in many places under the title of "reconciler of sinners," thanks especially to the Missionaries of Our Lady of La Salette.

Hence, if Mass is celebrated during Lent in honor of our Lady, especially in sanctuaries where the faithful gather in large numbers for the sacrament of penance, this formulary is appropriate, extolling as it does the "mercies" of God "to every creature" (Ent Ant, A, Psalm 145:9) and honoring the Blessed Virgin for her "heart of compassion for sinners" (Pref).

Except for the preface, almost all the Mass texts are taken from the *Missa propria beatae Mariae Virginis Reconciliatricis peccatorum,* Vatican Polyglot Press, 1978, pp. 4–6.

Entrance Antiphon

A **Gracious and merciful is the Lord, slow to anger, full of love. The Lord is good in every way, merciful to every creature.** *Psalm 145:8-9*

B **Hail, full of grace; you are called upon by sinners because you are merciful and look on our distress with compassion.**

OPENING PRAYER

Lord our God,
through the precious blood of your Son
you reconciled the world to yourself
and at the foot of his cross
you chose the Blessed Virgin Mary
to be the mother of reconciliation for sinners;
grant through her intercession
that we may obtain pardon for our sins.

We make our prayer through our Lord Jesus Christ,
your Son,
who lives and reigns with you and the Holy Spirit,
one God, for ever and ever.

PRAYER OVER THE GIFTS

Lord,
we offer you these gifts
of reconciliation and praise,
that through the intercession
of the Blessed Virgin Mary, refuge of sinners,
you may in your mercy pardon our sins
and steady our wavering hearts.

We ask this through Christ our Lord.

PREFACE **P 14** (Page 127)

Communion Antiphon

Glory and praise are yours, Mary: from you rose the sun of justice, Christ, our God.

PRAYER AFTER COMMUNION

Lord our God,
we have received the body and blood of your Son,
the sacrament of our reconciliation;
grant through the intercession
of the Blessed Virgin Mary
that this sacrament may bring us
the grace of your loving forgiveness
and the reward of eternal redemption.

We ask this through Christ our Lord.

EASTER SEASON

During the ''great Sunday,'' the fifty-day period in which with joyful exultation the Church celebrates the paschal mystery, the Roman liturgy also commemorates the Mother of Christ as she was filled with joy because of the resurrection of her Son and as she devoted herself to prayer with the apostles in trusting expectation of the gift of the Holy Spirit (see Acts 1:14). When, in fulfillment of its maternal role, the Church celebrates the sacraments of Christian initiation—which are paschal sacraments—it acknowledges the Blessed Virgin as the model of this maternal role. The Church also accepts the Mother of Christ as its exemplar and helper in the mission of proclaiming the Gospel that Christ entrusted to it after his resurrection from the dead (see Matthew 28:19-20).

15. THE BLESSED VIRGIN MARY AND THE RESURRECTION OF THE LORD

This Mass, except for the entrance antiphon and the preface, is taken from the *Roman Missal (Sacramentary),* Common of the Blessed Virgin Mary, for the Easter Season (MR, pp. 675–676), the texts of which are notable for their teaching and beauty.

The Mass celebrates the Lord's resurrection and the joy that flows from it:

—*to the whole world,* joy given by God the Father "by the resurrection of (his) Son, our Lord Jesus Christ" (OP); and so the day of the Lord's resurrection was a "day of light and life when the night of death" was ended and "the whole world (was to exult)" (Pref).

—*to the infant Church,* which trembled "with joy at seeing again its immortal Lord" (Pref, see Luke 24:41; John 20:20).

—*to the Virgin Mother,* whose heart was filled "with joy beyond all telling" at the resurrection of Christ (Pref).

The Church therefore greets the Virgin and invites her to rejoice: "Rejoice, Virgin Mother, for Christ has arisen from his grave" (Com Ant); "Rejoice, Mother of Light: Jesus, the sun of justice, overcoming the darkness of the tomb, sheds his radiance over the whole world" (Ent Ant); "Hail, holy Mary, as you stood by the cross in sorrow, you bore the sufferings of your Son, but now you are filled with serenity and joy" *(All).*

The Blessed Virgin, who conceived her Son in faith, and in faith looked forward to his resurrection (see Pref), is the model of faith by which disciples acknowledge Christ, the child conceived by the Virgin Mary, to be truly God and truly human, and through the saving power of the resurrection look forward to eternal happiness (see PAC).

Entrance Antiphon

Rejoice, Mother of Light: Jesus, the sun of justice, overcoming the darkness of the tomb, sheds his radiance over the whole world, alleluia.

OPENING PRAYER

O God,
who gave joy to the world
by the resurrection of your Son, our Lord Jesus Christ,
grant that through the prayer of his mother, the Virgin Mary,
we may receive the true and lasting joys of life.

We ask this through our Lord Jesus Christ, your Son,
who lives and reigns with you and the Holy Spirit,
one God, for ever and ever.

PRAYER OVER THE GIFTS

O God,
as we celebrate this memorial of the Virgin Mary,
we offer you our gifts and prayers,
that we may be sustained by the love of Christ,
who offered himself as a spotless victim on the cross
and who is Lord for ever and ever.

PREFACE **P 15** (Page 128)

Communion Antiphon

Rejoice, Virgin Mother, for Christ has arisen from his grave, alleluia.

PRAYER AFTER COMMUNION

**Lord God,
we profess as truly God and truly human
the child conceived by the Virgin Mary.
Seal in our hearts the mysteries of true faith
and through the saving power of the resurrection
guide us to eternal happiness.**

We ask this through Christ our Lord.

16. HOLY MARY, FOUNTAIN OF LIGHT AND LIFE

The sacraments of Christian initiation, which are properly celebrated at the Easter Vigil, fashion the catechumens in the likeness of Christ: in the waters of baptism they are made children of God, through the anointing and laying on of hands they are filled with the Holy Spirit, and through the heavenly bread and wine of the eucharist they become one body with Christ.

The Fathers of the Church, however, frequently teach us that the mysteries of Christ, which the Church, our virgin mother, celebrates in the sacraments of Christian initiation, were "accomplished" in Mary, the Virgin Mother (Pref): the Spirit who sanctifies the womb of the Church— that is, the font of baptism—to bring forth children of God, sanctified Mary's womb so that she might bring forth the firstborn of many brothers and sisters (see Hebrews 2:11-15); the same Spirit who, on the day of Pentecost, came down upon the Blessed Virgin with an abundance of gifts, comes down from heaven upon the newly baptized in the celebration of the sacrament of confirmation; the body and blood that Christ offered on the altar of the cross for the life of the world and that the Church offers daily in the eucharistic sacrifice are the same body and blood that the Blessed Virgin Mary brought forth for our salvation.

This Mass commemorates the maternal role of both the Church and the Blessed Virgin in relation to the faithful. The motherhood of Mary is prior to the motherhood of the Church as type and model (see LG, no. 63).

The texts of the Mass celebrate our Lady as:

—*the Virgin Mother* (OP, see Pref) who, "overshadowed by the Holy Spirit" (Com Ant), became the mother of Christ, the bread of life (see John 6:35), by whom the faithful are nourished in the Church.

—*the mother of light* (Ent Ant), because she brought forth Christ, the light of the world (see John 12:46; Gos A, John 12:44-50).

—*the model of the Church* (Ent Ant), because the Church is itself a virgin and brings "to new birth in the chaste waters of baptism a people of faith" (Ent Ant), and "in imitation of the mother of Christ" makes its eucharistic offering (POG); and because those things "accomplished in sign through the sacraments of the Church" were "accomplished already in the Blessed Virgin" (Pref).

—*the sanctuary of the mysteries of God* (Com Ant), because she carried in her "virginal womb" Christ, the sacrament of the Father: in Christ are hidden all the treasures of salvation and grace, and through him the face of the Father is revealed to us (see Luke 10:22; John 14:9).

This formulary, with its echoes of the Easter Vigil liturgy, is appropriately used on Saturdays of the Easter season when, for a reasonable cause and in accordance with liturgical law, Mass is celebrated in honor of the Blessed Virgin Mary.

Entrance Antiphon

Hail, mother of light: a virgin, you gave birth to Christ, and became the model of the Church, our mother, bringing to new birth in the chaste waters of baptism a people of faith, alleluia.

OPENING PRAYER

**Lord,
from the chaste womb of the baptismal font
the Church, our mother, has given to children of this earth
a new birth as children of heaven.**

**Grant that through the life-giving Gospel
and your grace-filled sacraments
the Church may form its daughters and sons
in the likeness of Christ, its founder,
who was born of a Virgin Mother
as the firstborn of many brothers and sisters
and the Savior of the whole human race
and who lives and reigns with you and the Holy Spirit,
one God, for ever and ever.**

PRAYER OVER THE GIFTS

**All-holy Father,
receive this offering
which the Church, our virginal mother,
makes in imitation of the mother of Christ,
so that, gathered into unity
from every people and nation,
the Church may become one body,
living by the one Spirit.**

We ask this through Christ our Lord.

PREFACE **P 16** (Page 129)

Communion Antiphon

Blessed are you, Virgin Mary: you were overshadowed by the Holy Spirit and bore in your virginal womb the Son of the eternal Father and so became the sanctuary of the mysteries of God, alleluia.

PRAYER AFTER COMMUNION

**Lord our God,
fill with the Spirit of Christ
those you have nourished with his body,
so that our actions may always be guided
by that same Spirit,
who shines upon the pathways of the Church
and who sanctified the entire life of the Virgin Mother.**

We ask this through Christ our Lord.

17. OUR LADY OF THE CENACLE

Our Lady of the Cenacle is honored in the liturgy of several dioceses and religious families, especially in the Congregation of the Sisters of Our Lady of the Cenacle, founded by St. Therese Couderc (d. 1885).

The Church has come to see in our Lady, present at the first gathering of Christ's disciples (Ent Ant, see Acts 1:14), a mother cherishing the infant Church in her love and the supreme example of prayer in oneness of heart.

In this Mass formulary the Church gives glory to the Father in heaven for his gift of the Holy Spirit. Our Lady is here presented as:

—*the Virgin filled with the Holy Spirit:* God has poured out on her in abundance "the gifts of the Holy Spirit" (OP). The one "who was overshadowed by the Spirit at the incarnation of the Word is once more filled with (this) Gift from on high at the birth of God's new people" (Pref);

—*model for the Church:* above all, she is the model of prayer, for God has given us a wonderful example of prayer in the Church at its beginning (see Pref), namely, the mother of Jesus as she prays with the apostles in oneness of mind and heart (see Pref; see Ent Ant, Acts 1:14, OP). The one "who waited in prayer for the coming of Christ is still at prayer as she calls upon the promised Paraclete" (Pref). A model, too, of harmony, unity, and peace (see Pref, PAC); of obedience to the voice of the Holy Spirit (see POG); of watchfulness in waiting for the Second Coming of Christ (see Pref); of faithful observance of the word of God (see *All,* Luke 2:19) and eagerness to sow its seed.

Entrance Antiphon

With one heart the disciples continued steadfast in prayer with Mary, the mother of Jesus, alleluia. *See Acts 1:14*

OPENING PRAYER

Lord our God,
as the Blessed Virgin was at prayer with the apostles
you poured out on her in abundance
the gifts of the Holy Spirit;
grant through her intercession
that we too, being filled with the same Spirit,
may persevere with one mind in prayer
and bring to the world around us
the good news of salvation.

We make our prayer through our Lord Jesus Christ,
your Son,
who lives and reigns with you and the Holy Spirit,
one God, for ever and ever.

PRAYER OVER THE GIFTS

All-holy Father,
receive these gifts from joyful hearts
and grant that we may follow closely
the example of the Blessed Virgin Mary
by obeying the voice of the Spirit
and seeking to praise your glory in all things.

We ask this through Christ our Lord.

PREFACE **P 17** (Page 131)

Communion Antiphon

The disciples continued steadfast in the teaching of the apostles, in communion of spirit, in the breaking of bread, and in the practice of prayer, alleluia. *Acts 2:42*

PRAYER AFTER COMMUNION

Lord God,
you have fed your holy people
with the one bread of life;
renew us by the one gift of the Holy Spirit
and grant that under the protection of the Blessed Virgin
we may work for the unity and peace of all those
for whom your Son offered himself
as the sacrifice of our redemption.

We ask this through Christ our Lord.

18. THE BLESSED VIRGIN MARY, QUEEN OF APOSTLES

Many religious institutes and societies of apostolic life have as their patroness the Blessed Virgin Mary at prayer in the Cenacle and honor her liturgically under the title of ''queen of apostles.'' Prominent among these are the Society of the Catholic Apostolate, founded by Vincent Pallotti (d. 1850), the Pontifical Institute for Foreign Missions (P.I.M.E.), founded by Bishop Angelo Ramazzotti (d. 1861), the Pious Society of St. Paul for the Apostolate of the Press, and other institutes owing their origin to the Servant of God, Giacomo Alberione (d. 1971).

Many men and women in their apostolic and missionary zeal have noted the preeminent and ''royal'' position occupied by the mother of Jesus in the community of the early Church and have recognized the importance of her presence at the events of Pentecost in relation to the spread of the Gospel message.

This Mass, except for the preface, is taken from the *Proprium missarum Societatis Apostolatus Catholici,* Vatican Polyglot Press, 1972, pp. 3–6.

This formulary has great missionary value. The assembly of the faithful prays that the Church may spread ''the glory of (God's) name in our words and actions'' (OP), may ''spread throughout the world'' (POG), and ''may always advance in the way of salvation'' (PAC).

The preface celebrates God's ''plan of salvation,'' in which the Blessed Virgin, guided by the Holy Spirit, hastened with the message of salvation to the house of Elizabeth, and ''Peter and the other apostles,'' strengthened by the descent of the Spirit, moved out boldly from the Cenacle to preach the Gospel of Christ to all nations.

Entrance Antiphon

With one heart the disciples continued steadfast in prayer with Mary, the mother of Jesus, alleluia. *See Acts 1:14*

OPENING PRAYER

O God,
you gave the Holy Spirit to your apostles
as they joined in prayer with Mary, the mother of Jesus.
By the help of her prayers
grant us the gift of serving you faithfully
by spreading the glory of your name
in our words and actions.

We ask this through our Lord Jesus Christ, your Son,
who lives and reigns with you and the Holy Spirit,
one God, for ever and ever.

PRAYER OVER THE GIFTS

Lord,
in your goodness
and in answer to the prayers
of blessed Mary, ever virgin,
grant that our offering may enable the Church
to spread throughout the world
and reflect your glory
in a rich harvest of holiness.

We ask this through Christ our Lord.

PREFACE **P 18** (Page 133)

Communion Antiphon

Blessed is the womb of the Virgin Mary which bore the Son of the eternal Father, alleluia. *See Luke 11:27*

PRAYER AFTER COMMUNION

Lord our God,
your gifts of grace have renewed our strength
on this memorial of the Blessed Virgin Mary,
queen of apostles.

We pray that your people
may always advance in the way of salvation
by remaining faithful to your commands
and steadfast in serving others.

We ask this through Christ our Lord.

ORDER OF MASS

THE ORDER OF MASS

INTRODUCTORY RITES

The purpose of these rites is to help the assembled people become a worshiping community and to prepare them for listening to God's word and celebrating the eucharist. (See General Instruction, no. 24.)

ENTRANCE SONG

After the people have assembled, the priest and the ministers go to the altar while the entrance song is being sung.

When the priest comes to the altar, he makes the customary reverence with the ministers, kisses the altar and (if incense is used) incenses it. Then with the ministers, he goes to the chair.

GREETING

After the entrance song, the priest and the faithful remain standing and make the sign of the cross, as the priest says:

In the name of the Father, and of the Son, and of the Holy Spirit.

The people answer: **Amen.**

Then the priest, facing the people, extends his hands and greets all present with one of the following greetings:

a

The grace of our Lord Jesus Christ and the love of God and the fellowship of the Holy Spirit be with you all.

The people answer: **And also with you.**

b Or the priest says: **The grace and peace of God our Father and the Lord Jesus Christ be with you.**

The people answer: **Blessed be God, the Father of our Lord Jesus Christ.**

or:

And also with you.

c Or the priest says: **The Lord be with you.**

(Instead of the greeting, The Lord be with you, a bishop says, Peace be with you.)

The people answer: **And also with you.**

The priest, deacon, or other suitable minister may very briefly introduce the Mass of the day.

A. The rite of blessing and sprinkling holy water may be celebrated in all churches and chapels at all Sunday Masses celebrated on Sunday or on Saturday evening.

Or:

B. The penitential rite follows.

Or:

C. If the Mass is preceded by some part of a the liturgy of the hours, the penitential rite is omitted, and the *Kyrie* may be omitted. (See General Instruction on the Liturgy of the Hours, nos. 94–96.)

A. RITE OF BLESSING AND SPRINKLING OF HOLY WATER

When this rite is celebrated it takes the place of the penitential rite at the beginning of Mass. The *Kyrie* is also omitted.

After greeting the people the priest remains standing at his chair. A vessel containing the water to be blessed is placed before him. Facing, the people, he invites them to pray, using these or similar words:

Dear friends,
this water will be used
to remind us of our baptism.
Let us ask God to bless it
and to keep us faithful
to the Spirit he has given us.

After a brief silence, he joins his hands and continues:

a **God our Father,**
your gift of water
brings life and freshness to the earth;
it washes away our sins
and brings us eternal life.

We ask you now
to bless ✠ this water,
and to give us your protection on this day
which you have made your own.
Renew the living spring of your life
within us
and protect us in spirit and body,
that we may be free from sin
and come into your presence
to receive your gift of salvation.

We ask this through Christ our Lord.

b **Lord God almighty,**
creator of all life,
of body and soul,
we ask you to bless ✠ this water:
as we use it in faith
forgive our sins
and save us from all illness
and the power of evil.

Lord,
in your mercy
give us living water,
always springing up as a fountain of
salvation:
free us, body and soul, from every
danger,
and admit us to your presence
in purity of heart.

Grant this through Christ our Lord.

During the Easter season:

C **Lord God almighty,**
hear the prayers of your people:
we celebrate our creation and redemption.
Hear our prayers and bless ✠ this water
which gives fruitfulness to the fields,
and refreshment and cleansing to man.
You chose water to show your goodness
when you led your people to freedom
through the Red Sea
and satisfied their thirst in the desert
with water from the rock.
Water was the symbol used by the prophets
to foretell your new covenant with man.
You made the water of baptism holy
by Christ's baptism in the Jordan:
by it you give us a new birth
and renew us in holiness.
May this water remind us of our baptism,
and let us share the joy
of all who have been baptized at Easter.

We ask this through Christ our Lord.

Where it is customary, salt may be mixed with the holy water. The priest blesses the salt, saying:

Almighty God,
we ask you to bless ✠ this salt
as once you blessed the salt scattered over the water
by the prophet Elisha.
Wherever this salt and water are sprinkled,
drive away the power of evil,
and protect us always
by the presence of your Holy Spirit.

Grant this through Christ our Lord.

Then he pours the salt into the water in silence.

Taking the sprinkler, the priest sprinkles himself and his ministers, then the rest of the clergy and people. He may move through the church for the sprinkling of the people. Meanwhile, an antiphon or another appropriate song is sung.

When he returns to his place and the song is finished, the priest faces the people and, with joined hands, says:

May almighty God cleanse us of our sins,
and through the eucharist we celebrate
make us worthy to sit at his table
in his heavenly kingdom.

The people answer:

Amen.

When it is prescribed, the *Gloria* is sung or said:

B. PENITENTIAL RITE

After the introduction to the day's Mass, the priest invites the people to recall their sins and to repent of them in silence. He may use these or similar words:

a **As we prepare to celebrate the mystery of Christ's love,**
let us acknowledge our failures
and ask the Lord for pardon and strength.

b **Coming together as God's family,**
with confidence let us ask the Father's forgiveness,
for he is full of gentleness and compassion.

c **My brothers and sisters,**[1]
to prepare ourselves to celebrate the sacred mysteries,
let us call to mind our sins.

[1]At the discretion of the priest, other words which seem more suitable under the circumstances, such as friends, dearly beloved, brethren, may be used. This also applies to parallel instances in the liturgy.

A pause for silent reflection follows. After the silence, one of the following three forms is chosen:

a

All say: **I confess to almighty God,**
and to you, my brothers and sisters,
that I have sinned through my own fault

They strike their breast: **in my thoughts and in my words,**
in what I have done,
and in what I have failed to do;
and I ask blessed Mary, ever virgin,
all the angels and saints,
and you, my brothers and sisters,
to pray for me to the Lord our God.

The priest says the absolution: **May almighty God have mercy on us,**
forgive us our sins,
and bring us to everlasting life.

The people answer: **Amen.**

b

The priest says: **Lord, we have sinned against you:**
Lord, have mercy.

The people answer: **Lord, have mercy.**

Priest: **Lord, show us your mercy and love.**

People: **And grant us your salvation.**

The priest says the absolution: **May almighty God have mercy on us,**
forgive us our sins,
and bring us to everlasting life.

The people answer: **Amen.**

The priest (or other suitable minister) may make any one of the following invocations, in place of those given above:

C1

Priest: **You were sent to heal the contrite:**
Lord, have mercy.

The people answer: **Lord, have mercy.**

Priest: **You came to call sinners:**
Christ, have mercy.

People: **Christ, have mercy.**

Priest: **You plead for us at the right hand of the Father:**
Lord, have mercy.

People: **Lord, have mercy.**

The priest says the absolution: **May almighty God have mercy on us,**
forgive us our sins,
and bring us to everlasting life.

The people answer: **Amen.**

C2

Priest: **Lord Jesus, you came to gather the nations**
into the peace of God's kingdom:
Lord, have mercy.

The people answer: **Lord, have mercy.**

Priest: **You come in word and sacrament to strengthen us in holiness:**
Christ, have mercy.

People: **Christ, have mercy.**

The priest says the absolution: **May almighty God have mercy on us,**
forgive us our sins,
and bring us to everlasting life.

The people answer: **Amen.**

C3

Priest: **Lord Jesus, you are mighty God and Prince of Peace:**
Lord, have mercy.

The people answer: **Lord, have mercy.**

Priest: **Lord Jesus, you are Son of God and Son of Mary:**
Christ, have mercy.

People: **Christ, have mercy.**

Priest: **Lord Jesus, you are Word made flesh and splendor of the Father:**
Lord, have mercy.

People: **Lord, have mercy.**

The priest says the absolution: **May almighty God have mercy on us,**
forgive us our sins,
and bring us to everlasting life.

The people answer: **Amen.**

C4

Priest: **Lord Jesus, you came to reconcile us**
to one another and to the Father:
Lord, have mercy.

The people answer: **Lord, have mercy.**

Priest: **Lord Jesus, you heal the wounds of sin and division:**
Christ, have mercy.

People: **Christ, have mercy.**

Priest: **Lord Jesus, you intercede for us with your Father:**
Lord, have mercy.

Priest: **Lord, have mercy.**

The priest says the absolution: **May almighty God have mercy on us,**
forgive us our sins,
and bring us to everlasting life.

The people answer: **Amen.**

C5

Priest: **You raise the dead to life in the Spirit: Lord, have mercy.**

The people answer: **Lord, have mercy.**

Priest: **You bring pardon and peace to the sinner: Christ, have mercy.**

People: **Christ, have mercy.**

Priest: **You bring light to those in darkness: Lord, have mercy.**

People: **Lord, have mercy.**

The priest says the absolution: **May almighty God have mercy on us,**
forgive us our sins,
and bring us to everlasting life.

The people answer: **Amen.**

C6

Priest: **Lord Jesus, you raise us to new life: Lord, have mercy.**

The people answer: **Lord, have mercy.**

Priest: **Lord Jesus, you forgive us our sins: Christ, have mercy.**

People: **Christ, have mercy.**

Priest: **Lord Jesus, you feed us with your body and blood: Lord, have mercy.**

People: **Lord, have mercy.**

The priest says the absolution: **May almighty God have mercy on us,**
forgive us our sins,
and bring us to everlasting life.

The people answer: **Amen.**

C7

Priest: **Lord Jesus, you have shown us the way to the Father:**
Lord, have mercy.

The people answer: **Lord, have mercy.**

Priest: **Lord Jesus, you have given us the consolation of the truth:**
Christ, have mercy.

People: **Christ, have mercy.**

Priest: **Lord Jesus, you are the Good Shepherd,**
leading us into everlasting life:
Lord, have mercy.

People: **Lord, have mercy.**

The priest says the absolution: **May almighty God have mercy on us,**
forgive us our sins,
and bring us to everlasting life.

The people answer: **Amen.**

C8

Priest: **Lord Jesus, you healed the sick:**
Lord, have mercy.

The people answer: **Lord, have mercy.**

Priest: **Lord Jesus, you forgave sinners:**
Christ, have mercy.

People: **Christ, have mercy.**

Priest: **Lord Jesus, you give us yourself to heal us and bring us strength:**
Lord, have mercy.

People: **Lord, have mercy.**

The priest says the absolution: **May almighty God have mercy on us,**
forgive us our sins,
and bring us to everlasting life.

The people answer: **Amen.**

KYRIE

The invocations, Lord, have mercy or Kýrie, eléison, follow, unless they have already been used in one of the forms of the act of penance.

℣. **Lord, have mercy.**
℟. **Lord, have mercy.**

℣. **Christ, have mercy.**
℟. **Christ, have mercy.**

℣. **Lord, have mercy.**
℟. **Lord, have mercy.**

℣. **Kýrie, eléison.**
℟. **Kýrie, eléison.**

℣. **Christe, eléison.**
℟. **Christe, eléison.**

℣. **Kýrie, eléison.**
℟. **Kýrie, eléison.**

GLORIA

This hymn is said or sung on Sundays outside Advent and Lent, on solemnities and feasts, and in solemn local celebrations. (See General Instruction, no. 31.)

Glory to God in the highest,
and peace to his people on earth.

Lord God, heavenly King,
almighty God and Father,
we worship you, we give you thanks,
we praise you for your glory.
Lord Jesus Christ, only Son of the Father,
Lord God, Lamb of God,
you take away the sin of the world:
have mercy on us;
you are seated at the right hand of the Father:
receive our prayer.
For you alone are the Holy One,
you alone are the Lord,
you alone are the Most High,
Jesus Christ,
with the Holy Spirit,
in the glory of God the Father. Amen.

OPENING PRAYER

Afterwards the priest, with hands joined, sings or says:

Let us pray.

Priest and people pray silently for a while.

Then the priest extends his hands and sings or says the opening prayer, at the end of which the people respond:

Amen.

LITURGY OF THE WORD

FIRST READING

The reader goes to the lectern for the first reading. All sit and listen. To indicate the end, the reader adds:

The word of the Lord.

All respond: **Thanks be to God.**

RESPONSORIAL PSALM

The cantor sings or recites the psalm, and the people respond.

SECOND READING

When there is a second reading, it is read at the lectern as before. To indicate the end, the reader adds:

The word of the Lord.

All respond: **Thanks be to God.**

ALLELUIA OR GOSPEL ACCLAMATION

The alleluia or other chant follows. It is to be omitted if not sung. (General Instruction, no. 39; Introduction to the Lectionary [1981], no. 23)

GOSPEL

Meanwhile, if incense is used, the priest puts some in the censer. Then the deacon who is to proclaim the gospel bows to the priest and in a low voice asks his blessing:

Father, give me your blessing.

The priest says in a low voice:

The Lord be in your heart and on your lips
that you may worthily proclaim his gospel.
In the name of the Father, and of the Son,
✠ and of the Holy Spirit.

The deacon answers:

Amen.

If there is no deacon, the priest bows before the altar and says inaudibly:

Almighty God, cleanse my heart and my lips
that I may worthily proclaim your gospel.

Then the deacon (or the priest) goes to the lectern. He may be accompanied by ministers with incense and candles. He sings or says:

The Lord be with you.

The people answer:

And also with you.

The deacon (or priest) sings or says:

A reading from the holy gospel according to N.

He makes the sign of the cross on the book, and then on his forehead, lips and breast. The people respond:

Glory to you, Lord.

Then, if incense is used, the deacon (or priest) incenses the book, and proclaims the gospel.

At the end of the gospel, the deacon (or priest) adds:

The gospel of the Lord.

All respond:

Praise to you, Lord Jesus Christ.

Then he kisses the book, saying inaudibly:

May the words of the Gospel wipe away our sins.

HOMILY

A homily shall be given on all Sundays and holy days of obligation; it is recommended for other days.

PROFESSION OF FAITH

After the homily, the profession of faith is said on Sundays and solemnities; it may also be said in solemn local celebrations. (See General Instruction, no. 44.)

We believe in one God,
the Father, the Almighty,
maker of heaven and earth,
of all that is seen and unseen.

We believe in one Lord, Jesus Christ,
the only Son of God,
eternally begotten of the Father,
God from God, Light from Light,
true God from true God,
begotten, not made, one in Being with the Father.
Through him all things were made.
For us men and for our salvation
he came down from heaven:

All bow during these two lines:

by the power of the Holy Spirit
he was born of the Virgin Mary, and became man.
For our sake he was crucified under Pontius Pilate;
he suffered, died, and was buried.
On the third day he rose again
in fulfilment of the Scriptures;
he ascended into heaven
and is seated at the right hand of the Father.
He will come again in glory to judge the living and the dead,
and his kingdom will have no end.

We believe in the Holy Spirit, the Lord,
the giver of life,
who proceeds from the Father and the Son.
With the Father and the Son he is
worshiped and glorified.
He has spoken through the Prophets.
We believe in one holy catholic and
apostolic Church.
We acknowledge one baptism for the
forgiveness of sins.
We look for the resurrection of the dead,
and the life of the world to come. Amen.

In celebrations of Masses with children, the Apostles' Creed may be said after the homily.[1]

I believe in God, the Father almighty,
creator of heaven and earth.

I believe in Jesus Christ, his only Son,
our Lord.
He was conceived by the power of
the Holy Spirit
and born of the Virgin Mary.
He suffered under Pontius Pilate,
was crucified, died, and was buried.
He descended to the dead.
On the third day he rose again.
He ascended into heaven,
and is seated at the right hand of
the Father.
He will come again to judge the living
and the dead.

I believe in the Holy Spirit,
the holy catholic Church,
the communion of saints,
the forgiveness of sins,
the resurrection of the body,
and the life everlasting. Amen.

GENERAL INTERCESSIONS

Then follow the general intercessions (prayer of the faithful). The priest presides at the prayer. With a brief introduction, he invites the people to pray; after the intentions he says the concluding prayer.

It is desirable that the intentions be announced by the deacon, cantor, or other person. (See General Instruction, no. 47.)

[1]Directory for Masses with Children, no. 49.

LITURGY OF THE EUCHARIST

PREPARATION OF THE ALTAR AND THE GIFTS

After the liturgy of the word, the offertory song is begun. Meanwhile the ministers place the corporal, the purificator, the chalice, and the missal on the altar.

Sufficient hosts (and wine) for the communion of the faithful are to be prepared. It is most important that the faithful should receive the body of the Lord in hosts consecrated at the same Mass and should share the cup when it is permitted. Communion is thus a clearer sign of sharing in the sacrifice which is actually taking place (General Instruction, no. 56h).

It is desirable that the participation of the faithful be expressed by members of the congregation bringing up the bread and wine for the celebration of the eucharist or other gifts for the needs of the Church and the poor.

The priest, standing at the altar, takes the paten with the bread and, holding it slightly raised above the altar, says inaudibly:

Blessed are you, Lord, God of all creation.
Through your goodness we have this bread to offer,
which earth has given and human hands have made.
It will become for us the bread of life.

Then he places the paten with the bread on the corporal.

If no offertory song is sung, the priest may say the preceding words in an audible voice; then the people may respond:

Blessed be God for ever.

The deacon (or the priest) pours the wine and a little water into the chalice, saying inaudibly:

By the mystery of this water and wine may we come to share in the divinity of Christ, who humbled himself to share in our humanity.

Then the priest takes the chalice and, holding it slightly raised above the altar, says inaudibly:

Blessed are you, Lord, God of all creation.
Through your goodness we have this wine to offer,
fruit of the vine and work of human hands.
It will become our spiritual drink.

Then he places the chalice on the corporal.

If no offertory song is sung, the priest may say the preceding words in an audible voice; then the people may respond:

Blessed be God for ever.

The priest bows and says inaudibly:

Lord God, we ask you to receive us and be pleased with the sacrifice we offer you with humble and contrite hearts.

He may now incense the offerings and the altar. Afterwards the deacon or a minister incenses the priest and people.

Next the priest stands at the side of the altar and washes his hands, saying inaudibly:

Lord, wash away my iniquity;
cleanse me from my sin.

Standing at the center of the altar, facing the people, he extends and then joins his hands, saying:

Pray, brethren,[1] **that our sacrifice**
may be acceptable to God, the almighty Father.

The people respond:

May the Lord accept the sacrifice at your hands
for the praise and glory of his name,
for our good, and the good of all his Church.

PRAYER OVER THE GIFTS

With hands extended, the priest sings or says the prayer over the gifts, at the end of which the people respond:

Amen.

[1]At the discretion of the priest, other words which seem more suitable under the circumstances, such as **friends, dearly beloved, my brothers and sisters,** may be used.

EUCHARISTIC PRAYER

The priest begins the eucharistic prayer. With hands extended he sings or says:

The people answer:

He lifts up his hands and continues:

The people:

With hands extended, he continues:

The people:

The priest continues the preface with hands extended.

ACCLAMATION

At the end of the preface, he joins his hands and, together with the people, concludes it by singing or saying aloud:

**Holy, holy, holy Lord, God of power
and might,
heaven and earth are full of your glory.
Hosanna in the highest.
Blessed is he who comes in the name of
the Lord.
Hosanna in the highest.**

In all Masses the priest may say the eucharistic prayer in an audible voice. In sung Masses he may sing those parts of the eucharistic prayer which may be sung in a concelebrated Mass.

In the first eucharistic prayer (the Roman canon) the words in brackets may be omitted.

PREFACES

MARY, CHOSEN DAUGHTER OF ISRAEL **P 1**

Our Lady is daughter of Adam, child of Abraham, branch of Jesse

℣. **The Lord be with you.**
℟. **And also with you.**

℣. **Lift up your hearts.**
℟. **We lift them up to the Lord.**

℣. **Let us give thanks to the Lord our God.**
℟. **It is right to give him thanks and praise.**

**Father, all-powerful and ever-living God,
we do well always and everywhere to give you thanks.**

**You chose the Blessed Virgin Mary
as the crown of Israel and the beginning of the Church,
to reveal to all peoples
that salvation is born from Israel
and that your new family springs from a chosen root.**

**She is by nature the daughter of Adam,
who by her sinlessness undid the sin of Eve.
She is by faith the true child of Abraham,
who first believed and so conceived.
She is by descent the branch from the root of Jesse,
bearing the flower that is Jesus Christ our Lord.**

**Through him the angels of heaven
offer their prayer of adoration
as they rejoice in your presence for ever.
May our voices be one with theirs
in their triumphant hymn of praise:**

**Holy, holy, holy Lord, God of power and might,
heaven and earth are full of your glory.
  Hosanna in the highest.
Blessed is he who comes in the name of the Lord.
  Hosanna in the highest.**

MARY AND THE ANNUNCIATION OF THE LORD **P 2**

The Blessed Virgin received the angel's message in faith

℣. **The Lord be with you.**
℟. **And also with you.**

℣. **Lift up your hearts.**
℟. **We lift them up to the Lord.**

℣. **Let us give thanks to the Lord our God.**
℟. **It is right to give him thanks and praise.**

**Father, all-powerful and ever-living God,
we do well always and everywhere to give you thanks
through Jesus Christ our Lord.**

**He came to save humankind by becoming human himself.
The Virgin Mary, receiving the angel's message in faith,
conceived by the power of the Spirit
and bore your Son in purest love.
In Christ, the eternal truth,
your promise to Israel came true.
In Christ, the hope of all peoples,
our hope was realized beyond all expectation.**

**Through Christ the angels of heaven
offer their prayer of adoration
as they rejoice in your presence for ever.
May our voices be one with theirs
in their triumphant hymn of praise:**

**Holy, holy, holy Lord, God of power and might,
heaven and earth are full of your glory.
  Hosanna in the highest.
Blessed is he who comes in the name of the Lord.
  Hosanna in the highest.**

THE VISITATION OF THE BLESSED VIRGIN MARY **P 3**

Holy Mary, blessed for her belief in the promise of salvation

℣. **The Lord be with you.**
℟. **And also with you.**

℣. **Lift up your hearts.**
℟. **We lift them up to the Lord.**

℣. **Let us give thanks to the Lord our God.**
℟. **It is right to give him thanks and praise.**

Father, all-powerful and ever-living God,
we do well always and everywhere to give you thanks
through Jesus Christ our Lord.

By your Holy Spirit
you inspired Elizabeth
to reveal the surpassing honor
you have given to the Blessed Virgin Mary.

Mary is rightly hailed as blessed
because she believed in your promise of salvation;
in her act of loving service
she is greeted as mother of the Lord
by the mother of Christ's herald.

We make our own the canticle of joy
on the lips of God's Virgin Mother,
and in our lowliness we too proclaim your greatness
in the never-ending hymn
of the whole company of angels and saints
as they cry out:

Holy, holy, holy Lord, God of power and might,
heaven and earth are full of your glory.
  Hosanna in the highest.
Blessed is he who comes in the name of the Lord.
  Hosanna in the highest.

MARY, MOTHER OF GOD

P 4

Holy Mary rejoiced because as a virgin she gave birth to the Redeemer

℣. **The Lord be with you.**
℟. **And also with you.**

℣. **Lift up your hearts.**
℟. **We lift them up to the Lord.**

℣. **Let us give thanks to the Lord our God.**
℟. **It is right to give him thanks and praise.**

Father, all-powerful and ever-living God,
we do well always and everywhere to give you thanks.

By a wonderful and inexpressible mystery
the Blessed Virgin conceived your only Son
and bore in her pure womb the Lord of heaven.

She who knew not man becomes a mother,
she who has given birth remains a virgin.
What joy is hers at your twofold gift:
she is full of wonder at her virgin-motherhood
and full of joy at giving birth to the Redeemer.

Through him the angels of heaven
offer their prayer of adoration
as they rejoice in your presence for ever.
May our voices be one with theirs
in their triumphant hymn of praise:

Holy, holy, holy Lord, God of power and might,
heaven and earth are full of your glory.
  Hosanna in the highest.
Blessed is he who comes in the name of the Lord.
  Hosanna in the highest.

MARY, MOTHER OF THE SAVIOR **P 5**

The Savior comes forth from Mary as the Bridegroom of the Church

℣. **The Lord be with you.**
℟. **And also with you.**

℣. **Lift up your hearts.**
℟. **We lift them up to the Lord.**

℣. **Let us give thanks to the Lord our God.**
℟. **It is right to give him thanks and praise.**

**Father, all-powerful and ever-living God,
we do well always and everywhere to give you thanks
especially as we celebrate this holy season (of Christmas).**

**When Mary brought forth her child
from the secret shrine of her virginal womb
you revealed as a light for all nations
the sign and source of our salvation,
your Son, Jesus Christ.**

**Like the rising sun,
the Bridegroom of the Church
has dawned upon us
to rescue us from darkness and the shadow of death
and to make us a kingdom of unfailing light.**

**In our joy we sing to your glory
with all the choirs of angels:**

**Holy, holy, holy Lord, God of power and might,
heaven and earth are full of your glory.
  Hosanna in the highest.
Blessed is he who comes in the name of the Lord.
  Hosanna in the highest.**

MARY AND THE EPIPHANY OF THE LORD P 6

Christ is revealed to the world through the ministry of the Virgin

℣. **The Lord be with you.**
℟. **And also with you.**

℣. **Lift up your hearts.**
℟. **We lift them up to the Lord.**

℣. **Let us give thanks to the Lord our God.**
℟. **It is right to give him thanks and praise.**

Father, all-powerful and ever-living God,
we do well always and everywhere to give you thanks.

Through the ministry of the Blessed Virgin
you draw the families of all peoples
to faith in the Gospel.

The shepherds, bathed in your glory
and enlightened by choirs of angels,
acknowledged Christ as the Savior
and became the firstfruits of the Church
from the people of Israel.

The wise men, inspired by grace
and led by a shining star,
entered a lowly house,
found the child with his mother,
and, as the firstfruits of the Church from the Gentiles,
worshiped him as God,
proclaimed him as King,
and acknowledged him as Redeemer.

Through him the angels of heaven
offer their prayer of adoration
as they rejoice in your presence for ever.
May our voices be one with theirs
in their triumphant hymn of praise:

Holy, holy, holy Lord, God of power and might . . .

MARY AND THE PRESENTATION OF THE LORD P 7

Our Lady is the handmaid of God's plan of salvation

℣. **The Lord be with you.**
℟. **And also with you.**

℣. **Lift up your hearts.**
℟. **We lift them up to the Lord.**

℣. **Let us give thanks to the Lord our God.**
℟. **It is right to give him thanks and praise.**

Father all-holy,
we do well always to glorify you
and give you thanks,
as we celebrate this memorial of the Blessed Virgin Mary.

She is the virgin daughter of Zion
who, in fulfillment of the Law,
presents to you her Son,
the glory of your people Israel
and the light of all nations.

She is the Virgin,
the handmaid of your plan of salvation,
who presents to you the spotless Lamb,
to be sacrificed on the altar of the cross
for our salvation.

She is the Virgin Mother
who rejoices in this child of blessing,
is saddened by the prophecy of Simeon,
but who exults that your people
go out to meet their Savior.

**Lord, we see your providence
as Son and Mother are united
in the one undivided love,
in the one shared suffering,
in the single will to do what pleases you.**

**In our joy we sing to your glory
with all the choirs of angels:**

**Holy, holy, holy Lord, God of power and might,
heaven and earth are full of your glory.
Hosanna in the highest.
Blessed is he who comes in the name of the Lord.
Hosanna in the highest.**

OUR LADY OF NAZARETH **P 8**

The daily life of our Lady in the home at Nazareth

℣. **The Lord be with you.**
℟. **And also with you.**

℣. **Lift up your hearts.**
℟. **We lift them up to the Lord.**

℣. **Let us give thanks to the Lord our God.**
℟. **It is right to give him thanks and praise.**

Father all-holy,
we do well always to glorify you
and give you thanks
on this celebration of the glorious Virgin Mary.

At Nazareth she receives with faith
the message of Gabriel
and becomes the mother of your Son,
begotten by you before the ages,
now born into this world of time
as our Savior and our brother.

At Nazareth too,
in loving communion with her Son,
she watches over the growing Church
in the person of her child
and hands on to us
the shining example of her life.

In the holy house of Nazareth,
as the first disciple of her Son,
she receives the message of the Gospel,
treasures it in her heart,
and reflects on it in her mind.

**At Nazareth also this purest of virgins,
united with Joseph, the just man,
in an unbreakable bond of chaste love,
praises you in song,
worships you in silence,
honors you by her daily life,
and gives you glory as she cares for her family.**

**Now, with all the saints and angels,
we praise you for ever:**

**Holy, holy, holy Lord, God of power and might,
heaven and earth are full of your glory.
  Hosanna in the highest.
Blessed is he who comes in the name of the Lord.
  Hosanna in the highest.**

OUR LADY OF CANA

P 9

Our Lady tells the attendants to do what her Son commands

℣. **The Lord be with you.**
℟. **And also with you.**

℣. **Lift up your hearts.**
℟. **We lift them up to the Lord.**

℣. **Let us give thanks to the Lord our God.**
℟. **It is right to give him thanks and praise.**

Father all-holy,
we do well always to glorify you
and give you thanks
on this celebration of the glorious Virgin Mary.

With loving care for the bridegroom and his bride
she turns to her Son for help
and tells the servants to do what he commands.
Water is changed into wine,
the wedding guests rejoice,
as Christ foreshadows the wedding feast
that is his daily gift to his Bride, the Church.

In this great sign
the presence of the Messiah is proclaimed,
the outpouring of the Holy Spirit is foretold,
and the hour of salvation is foreshadowed
when Christ will clothe himself
with the royal robes of his passion
to shed his blood on the cross
for his Bride, the Church.

Through him the angels of heaven
offer their prayer of adoration
as they rejoice in your presence for ever.
May our voices be one with theirs
in their triumphant hymn of praise:

Holy, holy, holy Lord, God of power and might . . .

MARY, DISCIPLE OF THE LORD

P 10

How blessed is Mary, disciple of the incarnate Word!

℣. **The Lord be with you.**
℟. **And also with you.**

℣. **Lift up your hearts.**
℟. **We lift them up to the Lord.**

℣. **Let us give thanks to the Lord our God.**
℟. **It is right to give him thanks and praise.**

Father, all-powerful and ever-living God,
we do well always and everywhere to give you thanks
through Jesus Christ our Lord.

His mother, the Virgin Mary in her glory,
is rightly called blessed,
for she received your Son in her virginal womb,
but she is even more blessed
because, as a disciple of the incarnate Word,
she eagerly sought to know your will
and faithfully carried it out.

With the whole company of angels
we praise you with one voice:

Holy, holy, holy Lord, God of power and might,
heaven and earth are full of your glory.
  Hosanna in the highest.
Blessed is he who comes in the name of the Lord.
  Hosanna in the highest.

MARY AT THE FOOT OF THE CROSS I

P 11

Mary remains faithful beside the cross of her Son

℣. **The Lord be with you.**
℟. **And also with you.**

℣. **Lift up your hearts.**
℟. **We lift them up to the Lord.**

℣. **Let us give thanks to the Lord our God.**
℟. **It is right to give him thanks and praise.**

Father, all-powerful and ever-living God,
we do well always and everywhere to give you thanks
through Jesus Christ our Lord.

In your loving providence
you decreed that Mary, the mother of your Son,
should stand faithfully beside his cross,
and so fulfill in her person
the prophecies of old,
and enrich the world
with her own witness of living faith.

At the cross the Blessed Virgin appears as the new Eve,
so that, as a woman shared in bringing death,
so a woman would share in restoring life.

At the cross with motherly love
she embraces her scattered children,
reunited through the death of Christ,
and she fulfills the mystery of the mother of Zion.

At the cross she stands
as the model of the Church, the Bride of Christ,
which draws inspiration from her courage
and keeps constant faith with its Bridegroom,
undaunted by peril and unbroken by persecution.

In our joy we sing to your glory
with all the choirs of angels:

Holy, holy, holy Lord, God of power and might . . .

MARY AT THE FOOT OF THE CROSS II **P 12**

By a gift of God's love our Lady shared in the passion of her Son

℣. **The Lord be with you.**
℟. **And also with you.**

℣. **Lift up your hearts.**
℟. **We lift them up to the Lord.**

℣. **Let us give thanks to the Lord our God.**
℟. **It is right to give him thanks and praise.**

**Father, all-powerful and ever-living God,
we do well always and everywhere to give you thanks
through Jesus Christ our Lord.**

**In your divine wisdom
you planned the redemption of the human race
and decreed that the new Eve
should stand by the cross of the new Adam:
as she became his mother
by the power of the Holy Spirit,
so, by a new gift of your love,
she was to be a partner in his passion,
and she who had given him birth
without the pains of childbirth
was to endure the greatest of pains
in bringing forth to new life
the family of your Church.**

**Now, with angels and archangels,
and the whole company of heaven,
we sing the unending hymn of your praise:**

**Holy, holy, holy Lord, God of power and might,
heaven and earth are full of your glory.
Hosanna in the highest.
Blessed is he who comes in the name of the Lord.
Hosanna in the highest.**

THE COMMENDING OF THE BLESSED VIRGIN MARY P 13

Mary and John are commended to each other's care

℣. **The Lord be with you.**
℟. **And also with you.**

℣. **Lift up your hearts.**
℟. **We lift them up to the Lord.**

℣. **Let us give thanks to the Lord our God.**
℟. **It is right to give him thanks and praise.**

Father, all-powerful and ever-living God,
we do well always and everywhere to give you thanks.

At the foot of the cross of Jesus,
by his solemn and dying wish,
a deep bond of love is fashioned
between the Blessed Virgin Mary
and his faithful disciples:
the Mother of God is entrusted to the disciples
as their own mother,
and they receive her
as a precious inheritance from their Master.

She is to be for ever
the mother of those who believe,
and they will look to her
with great confidence in her unfailing protection.
She loves her Son in loving her children,
and in heeding what she says
they keep the words of their Master.

Through him the angels of heaven
offer their prayer of adoration
as they rejoice in your presence for ever.
May our voices be one with theirs
in their triumphant hymn of praise:

Holy, holy, holy Lord, God of power and might . . .

MARY, MOTHER OF RECONCILIATION **P 14**

The Blessed Virgin as the refuge of sinners and mother of reconciliation

℣. **The Lord be with you.**
℟. **And also with you.**

℣. **Lift up your hearts.**
℟. **We lift them up to the Lord.**

℣. **Let us give thanks to the Lord our God.**
℟. **It is right to give him thanks and praise.**

Father, all-powerful and ever-living God,
we do well always and everywhere to give you thanks
in all things and for all things
and to proclaim your mighty deeds.

In your infinite goodness
you do not abandon those who stray from you,
but in marvelous ways you call them back to your love:
you gave the Blessed Virgin Mary,
sinless as she was,
a heart of compassion for sinners;
seeing her love as their mother,
they turn to her with trust
as they ask your forgiveness;
seeing her beauty of spirit,
they seek to turn away from sin in its ugliness;
taking to heart her words and example,
they learn to keep your Son's commandments.

Through him the angels of heaven
offer their prayer of adoration
as they rejoice in your presence for ever.
May our voices be one with theirs
in their triumphant hymn of praise:

Holy, holy, holy Lord, God of power and might . . .

MARY AND THE RESURRECTION OF THE LORD P 15

The Blessed Virgin looked forward in faith to the resurrection of her Son

℣. **The Lord be with you.**
℟. **And also with you.**

℣. **Lift up your hearts.**
℟. **We lift them up to the Lord.**

℣. **Let us give thanks to the Lord our God.**
℟. **It is right to give him thanks and praise.**

Father, all-powerful and ever-living God,
we do well always and everywhere to give you thanks.

At the resurrection of your Anointed One
you filled the heart of the Blessed Virgin
with joy beyond all telling
and wonderfully exalted her faith.

For it was in faith
that she conceived your Son,
it was in faith
that she awaited his resurrection.

In the strength of faith
she waited for that day of light and life
when the night of death would be ended,
the whole world would exult,
and the infant Church tremble with joy
at seeing again its immortal Lord.

Through him the angels of heaven
offer their prayer of adoration
as they rejoice in your presence for ever.
May our voices be one with theirs
in their triumphant hymn of praise:

Holy, holy, holy Lord, God of power and might . . .

MARY, FOUNTAIN OF LIGHT AND LIFE **P 16**

The role of the Blessed Virgin in the sacraments of Christian initiation

℣. **The Lord be with you.**
℟. **And also with you.**

℣. **Lift up your hearts.**
℟. **We lift them up to the Lord.**

℣. **Let us give thanks to the Lord our God.**
℟. **It is right to give him thanks and praise.**

Father, all-powerful and ever-living God,
we do well always and everywhere to give you thanks.

By the marvelous gift of your loving kindness
you decreed that the mysteries
accomplished already in the Blessed Virgin
should be accomplished in sign
through the sacraments of the Church:
for from the baptismal font the Church brings to birth
new sons and daughters conceived in fruitful virginity
through faith and the Holy Spirit.

These newborn children the Church anoints
with the precious oil of sacred chrism,
so that the Spirit,
who filled the Blessed Virgin
with an abundance of gifts,
may come down to bless them
with an outpouring of grace.

Each day the Church also prepares for its children
the table where it nourishes them with the bread of heaven,
born of the Virgin Mary for the life of the world:
Jesus Christ our Lord.

Through him the angels of heaven
offer their prayer of adoration
as they rejoice in your presence for ever.
May our voices be one with theirs
in their triumphant hymn of praise:

Holy, holy, holy Lord, God of power and might,
heaven and earth are full of your glory.
  Hosanna in the highest.
Blessed is he who comes in the name of the Lord.
  Hosanna in the highest.

OUR LADY OF THE CENACLE

P 17

*The Blessed Virgin, at prayer with the apostles,
awaits the coming of the Paraclete*

℣. **The Lord be with you.**
℟. **And also with you.**

℣. **Lift up your hearts.**
℟. **We lift them up to the Lord.**

℣. **Let us give thanks to the Lord our God.**
℟. **It is right to give him thanks and praise.**

**Father, all-powerful and ever-living God,
we do well always and everywhere to give you thanks.**

**How wonderful is the example you have given us
of harmony and prayer in the Church at its beginning:
you show us the mother of Jesus
as she prays with the apostles
in oneness of mind and heart.**

**She who waited in prayer for the coming of Christ
is still at prayer
as she calls upon the promised Paraclete;
she who was overshadowed by the Spirit
at the incarnation of the Word
is once more filled with your Gift from on high
at the birth of God's new people.**

**As she keeps vigil in prayer,
her heart on fire with love,
she is the model of the Church,
enriched by the gifts of the Spirit
and keeping watch for the Second Coming of Christ.**

**Through him the angels of heaven
offer their prayer of adoration
as they rejoice in your presence for ever.
May our voices be one with theirs
in their triumphant hymn of praise:**

**Holy, holy, holy Lord, God of power and might,
heaven and earth are full of your glory.
Hosanna in the highest.
Blessed is he who comes in the name of the Lord.
Hosanna in the highest.**

MARY, QUEEN OF APOSTLES

P 18

The Blessed Virgin as queen of apostles

℣. **The Lord be with you.**
℟. **And also with you.**

℣. **Lift up your hearts.**
℟. **We lift them up to the Lord.**

℣. **Let us give thanks to the Lord our God.**
℟. **It is right to give him thanks and praise.**

**Father, all-powerful and ever-living God,
we do well always and everywhere to give you thanks
on this memorial of the Blessed Virgin Mary,
the first to proclaim Christ,
even before the apostles.
Guided by the Holy Spirit,
she hastened to bring her Son to John,
that he might be sanctified and filled with joy.
It was the same Spirit
who made Peter and the other apostles
fearless in preaching the Gospel to all nations,
with its saving message of life in Christ.**

**In our own day the Blessed Virgin
inspires by her example new preachers of the Gospel,
cherishes them with a mother's love,
and sustains them by her unceasing prayer,
so that they may bring the Good News of Christ the Savior
to all the world.**

**With all the saints and angels
we praise you for ever:**

**Holy, holy, holy Lord, God of power and might,
heaven and earth are full of your glory.
  Hosanna in the highest.
Blessed is he who comes in the name of the Lord.
  Hosanna in the highest.**

MARY, MOTHER OF THE LORD **P 19**

The Mother of the Lord is entrusted with the distribution of divine grace

℣. **The Lord be with you.**
℟. **And also with you.**

℣. **Lift up your hearts.**
℟. **We lift them up to the Lord.**

℣. **Let us give thanks to the Lord our God.**
℟. **It is right to give him thanks and praise.**

Father, all-powerful and ever-living God,
we do well always and everywhere to give you thanks.

In the mother of your Son
you showed the wonders of your power
and through her you still continue
to accomplish in us our salvation.
In your wisdom and love
she fulfills a mother's role
in the household of the Church
and is entrusted with the distribution of grace.
Through her words you instruct us,
through her example you draw us to follow her Son,
through her prayers you grant us forgiveness.

With thankful praise,
in company with the choirs of heaven,
we glorify your power
as we sing with one voice:

Holy, holy, holy Lord, God of power and might,
heaven and earth are full of your glory.
  Hosanna in the highest.
Blessed is he who comes in the name of the Lord.
  Hosanna in the highest.

MARY, THE NEW EVE

P 20

Mary, the new Eve, is the first disciple of the New Law

℣. **The Lord be with you.**
℟. **And also with you.**

℣. **Lift up your hearts.**
℟. **We lift them up to the Lord.**

℣. **Let us give thanks to the Lord our God.**
℟. **It is right to give him thanks and praise.**

**Father, all-powerful and ever-living God,
we do well always and everywhere to give you thanks
through Jesus Christ, our Lord.**

**You gave to Christ, author of the New Covenant,
the Blessed Virgin Mary as his mother and companion
and you made her the firstfruits of your new people.**

**Conceived without stain,
enriched by gifts of grace,
she is indeed the new woman,
the first disciple of the New Law.**

**She is a woman who finds joy in your service,
who is attentive to the voice of the Spirit,
who is always ready to obey your word.**

**She is a woman blest for her faith,
a woman blest in her child,
a woman raised up from among the lowly.**

**She is a woman standing firm in adversity,
keeping faith by the cross of her Son,
entering into glory at the end of her days.**

**With the whole company of the angels
we praise you with one voice:**

Holy, holy, holy Lord, God of power and might . . .

THE HOLY NAME OF MARY

P 21

Our Lady is the temple of God's glory

℣. **The Lord be with you.**
℟. **And also with you.**

℣. **Lift up your hearts.**
℟. **We lift them up to the Lord.**

℣. **Let us give thanks to the Lord our God.**
℟. **It is right to give him thanks and praise.**

**Father, all-powerful and ever-living God,
we do well always and everywhere to give you thanks
through Jesus Christ our Lord.
In no other name is there salvation;
at his command every knee must bend,
in heaven, on earth, and under the earth.**

**But by your loving providence
the name of the Virgin Mary also
should echo and re-echo
on the lips of your faithful people
who turn to her with confidence
as their star of hope,
call on her as their mother
in time of danger,
and seek her protection
in their hour of need.**

**With thankful praise,
in company with the angels,
we glorify your power
as we sing with one voice:**

**Holy, holy, holy Lord, God of power and might,
heaven and earth are full of your glory.
Hosanna in the highest.
Blessed is he who comes in the name of the Lord.
Hosanna in the highest.**

MARY, HANDMAID OF THE LORD **P 22**

The Blessed Virgin, handmaid of the Lord,
was a servant of the mystery of redemption

℣. **The Lord be with you.**
℟. **And also with you.**

℣. **Lift up your hearts.**
℟. **We lift them up to the Lord.**

℣. **Let us give thanks to the Lord our God.**
℟. **It is right to give him thanks and praise.**

Father, all-powerful and ever-living God,
we do well always and everywhere to give you thanks.

In the Blessed Virgin Mary
you were especially pleased,
for by embracing your plan of salvation
she gave herself wholeheartedly
to the work of your Son
as a faithful servant of the mystery of redemption.

She who gave great service to Christ
was given great honor by you, his Father.
She who saw herself as your lowly handmaid
was raised up by you to reign as queen in glory
in the presence of your Son,
where she intercedes for us in her goodness
as the servant of your love.

Now with all the saints and angels,
we praise you for ever:

Holy, holy, holy Lord, God of power and might,
heaven and earth are full of your glory.
  Hosanna in the highest.
Blessed is he who comes in the name of the Lord.
  Hosanna in the highest.

MARY, TEMPLE OF THE LORD

P 23

Our Lady is a temple of God's glory without compare

℣. **The Lord be with you.**
℟. **And also with you.**

℣. **Lift up your hearts.**
℟. **We lift them up to the Lord.**

℣. **Let us give thanks to the Lord our God.**
℟. **It is right to give him thanks and praise.**

Father, all-powerful and ever-living God,
we do well always and everywhere to give you thanks.

By the grace of the Holy Spirit
you purify our hearts by your light
and sanctify them with your presence,
so that they become the dwelling-place of your glory.

But because of her obedience of faith
and the mystery of the incarnation
you made the Blessed Virgin your temple without compare:
a house of gold adorned by the Spirit
with every kind of virtue,
a royal palace resplendent
with the presence of the One who is the Truth,
the holy city, rejoicing in its streams of grace,
the ark of the New Covenant
enshrining the author of the New Law,
Jesus Christ our Lord.

Through him the angels of heaven
offer their prayer of adoration
as they rejoice in your presence for ever.
May our voices be one with theirs
in their triumphant hymn of praise:

Holy, holy, holy Lord, God of power and might . . .

MARY, SEAT OF WISDOM P 24

Wisdom has built himself a house in the chaste womb of Mary

℣. **The Lord be with you.**
℟. **And also with you.**

℣. **Lift up your hearts.**
℟. **We lift them up to the Lord.**

℣. **Let us give thanks to the Lord our God.**
℟. **It is right to give him thanks and praise.**

Father, all-powerful and ever-living God,
we do well always and everywhere to give you thanks
through Jesus Christ our Lord.

In your infinite goodness,
when the fullness of time had come,
you accomplished through the Blessed Virgin Mary
the mystery of our reconciliation planned before all ages.
Wisdom built himself a house
in the chaste womb of the Virgin Mary,
the Creator of time came to be born
in this world of time,
so that as the new Adam
he might undo the ancient inheritance of sin
and renew us in his own resplendent image.

With all the saints and angels
we praise you for ever:

Holy, holy, holy Lord, God of power and might,
heaven and earth are full of your glory.
Hosanna in the highest.
Blessed is he who comes in the name of the Lord.
Hosanna in the highest.

MARY, IMAGE AND MOTHER OF THE CHURCH I **P 25**

Mary is the image and mother of the Church

℣. **The Lord be with you.**
℟. **And also with you.**

℣. **Lift up your hearts.**
℟. **We lift them up to the Lord.**

℣. **Let us give thanks to the Lord our God.**
℟. **It is right to give him thanks and praise.**

Father, all-powerful and ever-living God,
we do well always and everywhere to give you thanks;
we especially praise you and proclaim your glory
as we honor the Blessed Virgin Mary.
She received your Word in the purity of her heart
and, conceiving in her virgin womb,
gave birth to our Savior
and so nurtured the Church at its very beginning.

She accepted God's parting gift of love
as she stood beneath the cross
and so became the mother of all those
who were brought to life
through the death of her only Son.

She joined her prayers with those of the apostles,
as together they awaited the coming of your Spirit,
and so became the perfect pattern of the Church at prayer.

Raised to the glory of heaven,
she cares for the pilgrim Church with a mother's love,
following its progress homeward
until the day of the Lord dawns in splendor.

Now, with all the angels and saints,
we proclaim your glory
and join in their unending hymn of praise:

Holy, holy, holy Lord, God of power and might . . .

MARY, IMAGE AND MOTHER OF THE CHURCH II **P 26**

Our Lady as an example of true worship

℣. **The Lord be with you.**
℟. **And also with you.**

℣. **Lift up your hearts.**
℟. **We lift them up to the Lord.**

℣. **Let us give thanks to the Lord our God.**
℟. **It is right to give him thanks and praise.**

Father, all-powerful and ever-living God,
we do well always and everywhere to give you thanks
through Jesus Christ our Lord.

In your infinite goodness
you have given to the virgin Church
the model of true worship in the Virgin Mary.

She is the Virgin who listens,
who embraces your words with joy,
treasuring them in the silence of her heart.

She is the Virgin of prayer,
who sings of your mercy in her canticle of praise,
who shows concern for the bridegroom and bride of Cana
and intercedes for them with her Son,
who prays with the apostles in oneness of mind and heart.

She is the Virgin Mother,
who gives birth to your Son
by the power of the Holy Spirit
and at the foot of the cross
is proclaimed as mother
of the people of the New Covenant.

**She is the Virgin who offers,
presenting the Firstborn in your temple
and sharing in his self-offering
beside the tree of everlasting life.**

**She is the Virgin who keeps vigil,
awaiting the resurrection of her Son
with unwavering hope
and looking forward to the coming of the Holy Spirit,
with steadfast faith.**

**In our joy we sing to your glory
with all the choirs of angels:**

**Holy, holy, holy Lord, God of power and might,
heaven and earth are full of your glory.
Hosanna in the highest.
Blessed is he who comes in the name of the Lord.
Hosanna in the highest.**

MARY, IMAGE AND MOTHER OF THE CHURCH III P 27

The Blessed Virgin is the resplendent image of the Church in its future glory

℣. **The Lord be with you.**
℟. **And also with you.**

℣. **Lift up your hearts.**
℟. **We lift them up to the Lord.**

℣. **Let us give thanks to the Lord our God.**
℟. **It is right to give him thanks and praise.**

Father, all-powerful and ever-living God,
we do well always and everywhere to give you thanks.

You have given the Blessed Virgin Mary to your Church
as the perfect image
of its role as mother
and of its future glory.
She is a virgin unsurpassed in purity of faith,
a bride joined to Christ
in an unbreakable bond of love
and united with him in his suffering.
She is a mother by the overshadowing of the Holy Spirit,
filled with loving concern for all her children.
She is a queen adorned with the jewels of grace,
robed with the sun and crowned with stars,
sharing eternally in the glory of her Lord.

Through him the angels of heaven
offer their prayer of adoration
as they rejoice in your presence for ever.
May our voices be one with theirs
in their triumphant hymn of praise:

Holy, holy, holy Lord, God of power and might,
heaven and earth are full of your glory.
  Hosanna in the highest.
Blessed is he who comes in the name of the Lord.
  Hosanna in the highest.

THE IMMACULATE HEART OF MARY **P 28**

The heart of Mary is the heart of one who lives by the New Law

℣. **The Lord be with you.**
℟. **And also with you.**

℣. **Lift up your hearts.**
℟. **We lift them up to the Lord.**

℣. **Let us give thanks to the Lord our God.**
℟. **It is right to give him thanks and praise.**

Father, all-powerful and ever-living God,
we do well always and everywhere to give you thanks
through Jesus Christ our Lord.

You gave the Blessed Virgin Mary
a wise and obedient heart,
that she might perfectly carry out your will,
a new and gentle heart,
in which you were well pleased
and on which you inscribed
the law of the New Covenant.

You gave her an undivided and pure heart,
that she might be worthy
to be the Virgin Mother of your Son
and to rejoice to see you for ever.
You gave her a steadfast and watchful heart,
so that she could endure without fear the sword of sorrow
and await in faith the resurrection of her Son.

With the whole company of the angels
we sing your praises
in their canticle of joy:

Holy, holy, holy Lord, God of power and might,
heaven and earth are full of your glory.
  Hosanna in the highest.
Blessed is he who comes in the name of the Lord.
  Hosanna in the highest.

MARY, QUEEN OF ALL CREATION **P 29**

The lowly handmaid of the Lord is exalted as queen of heaven

℣. **The Lord be with you.**
℟. **And also with you.**

℣. **Lift up your hearts.**
℟. **We lift them up to the Lord.**

℣. **Let us give thanks to the Lord our God.**
℟. **It is right to give him thanks and praise.**

**Father, all-powerful and ever-living God,
we do well always and everywhere to give you thanks
through Jesus Christ our Lord.**

**You are merciful and just,
scattering the proud and raising up the broken-hearted.
When your Son humbled himself and accepted death
you crowned him with glory and honor
and seated him at your right hand
as King of kings and Lord of lords.**

**When the Blessed Virgin, your lowly handmaid,
endured with patient suffering
the shame of her Son's crucifixion
you exalted her above all the choirs of angels
to reign with him in glory
and to intercede for all your children,
our advocate of grace
and the queen of all creation.**

**With the whole host of angels
we proclaim your greatness
as we praise you with one voice:**

**Holy, holy, holy Lord, God of power and might,
heaven and earth are full of your glory.
Hosanna in the highest.
Blessed is he who comes in the name of the Lord.
Hosanna in the highest.**

MARY, MOTHER AND MEDIATRIX OF GRACE **P 30**

The love the Blessed Virgin bestows as a mother

℣. **The Lord be with you.**
℟. **And also with you.**

℣. **Lift up your hearts.**
℟. **We lift them up to the Lord.**

℣. **Let us give thanks to the Lord our God.**
℟. **It is right to give him thanks and praise.**

**Father, all-powerful and ever-living God,
we do well always and everywhere to give you thanks
through Jesus Christ our Lord.
Truly God and truly human,
he was chosen by you
as the one mediator between you and the human family,
always living to make intercession for us.
In your wisdom and goodness
the Blessed Virgin Mary, the mother and companion
of the Redeemer,
was to have a maternal role in the Church:
of intercession and pardon,
of prayer and grace,
of reconciliation and peace.
The love that she bestows as a mother
is entirely the gift of Christ, the one mediator,
from whom alone she receives her power.**

**Her children, in their trials and fears,
turn with confidence to the Blessed Virgin,
calling to her as mother of mercy and handmaid of grace.**

**In our joy we sing to your glory
with all the choirs of angels:**

Holy, holy, holy Lord, God of power and might . . .

MARY, FOUNTAIN OF SALVATION **P 31**

The Blessed Virgin brought forth Jesus Christ, the fountain of living water

℣. **The Lord be with you.**
℟. **And also with you.**

℣. **Lift up your hearts.**
℟. **We lift them up to the Lord.**

℣. **Let us give thanks to the Lord our God.**
℟. **It is right to give him thanks and praise.**

Father, all-powerful and ever-living God,
we do well always and everywhere to give you thanks
and, as we celebrate the glory of the Blessed Virgin Mary,
to proclaim with fitting praise
the greatness of your name.

In the great mystery of the incarnation
the Holy Spirit overshadowed the Blessed Virgin
and she brought forth your eternal Word,
Jesus Christ, the fountain of living water,
from which all may satisfy their thirst
to be one with you in a communion of love.

The Church also provided for all the faithful
the waters flowing from Christ's side.
These are the rich, life-giving waters
served in the sacraments,
so that those who share in them with faith
may be filled with the Holy Spirit
and may find Christ, their Savior.

Through him the angels of heaven
offer their prayer of adoration
as they rejoice in your presence for ever.
May our voices be one with theirs
in their triumphant hymn of praise:

Holy, holy, holy Lord, God of power and might . . .

MARY, MOTHER AND TEACHER IN THE SPIRIT **P 32**

The Blessed Virgin, our mother, lovingly encourages her children and guides them by her example

℣. **The Lord be with you.**
℟. **And also with you.**

℣. **Lift up your hearts.**
℟. **We lift them up to the Lord.**

℣. **Let us give thanks to the Lord our God.**
℟. **It is right to give him thanks and praise.**

Father, all-powerful and ever-living God,
we do well always and everywhere to give you thanks
and, as we celebrate the memory of blessed Mary, ever virgin,
to praise, to bless, and to proclaim your holy name.

So intimately does she share in the mystery of Christ
that she is still a mother,
continuing to give you children with the Church,
encouraging them by her love,
and drawing them by her example
to pursue perfect charity.

She is the model
of all who live by the spirit of the Gospel;
as we look up to her in prayer
we learn from her mind
to love you above all things,
from her spirit
to be rapt in contemplation of your Word,
and from her heart
to serve the needs of others.

In our joy we sing to your glory
with all the choirs of angels:

Holy, holy, holy Lord, God of power and might . . .

MARY, MOTHER OF GOOD COUNSEL

P 33

Our Lady gave herself wholeheartedly to God's loving plan

℣. **The Lord be with you.**
℟. **And also with you.**

℣. **Lift up your hearts.**
℟. **We lift them up to the Lord.**

℣. **Let us give thanks to the Lord our God.**
℟. **It is right to give him thanks and praise.**

**Father, all-powerful and ever-living God,
we do well always and everywhere to give you thanks
through Jesus Christ our Lord.**

**How generously you poured out
the gifts of your Holy Spirit
upon the Blessed Virgin Mary
to make her worthy
to be the mother and companion of the Redeemer.**

**Enlightened by these gifts,
she sought your will unceasingly
and obeyed it with fidelity.
In her canticle of joy
she proclaimed the greatness of your mercy
and gave herself wholeheartedly
to your wise and loving plan
for renewing all things in Christ.**

**Through him the angels of heaven
offer their prayer of adoration
as they rejoice in your presence for ever.
May our voices be one with theirs
in their triumphant hymn of praise:**

Holy, holy, holy Lord, God of power and might . . .

MARY, CAUSE OF OUR JOY

P 34

The life of the Blessed Virgin, cause of our joy

℣. **The Lord be with you.**
℟. **And also with you.**

℣. **Lift up your hearts.**
℟. **We lift them up to the Lord.**

℣. **Let us give thanks to the Lord our God.**
℟. **It is right to give him thanks and praise.**

**Father, all-powerful and ever-living God,
we do well always and everywhere to give you thanks
and, as we honor the memory of the Blessed Virgin,
the daughter of your love,
to proclaim with fitting praise
the greatness of your name.**

**Her blessed birth
heralded joy for all the world.
Her virgin-motherhood
brought forth the true Light,
the source of all joy.
Her hidden life
brings light and warmth
to all the Churches of the world.
Her passing into glory
raised her to the heights of heaven,
where, as our sister and our mother,
she waits for us with loving care
until we too enjoy the vision of your glory for ever.**

**In our joy we sing to your glory
with all the choirs of angels:**

**Holy, holy, holy Lord, God of power and might,
heaven and earth are full of your glory.
  Hosanna in the highest.
Blessed is he who comes in the name of the Lord.
  Hosanna in the highest.**

MARY, PILLAR OF FAITH

P 35

Our Lady is the hope of the faithful, a pillar of faith

℣. **The Lord be with you.**
℟. **And also with you.**

℣. **Lift up your hearts.**
℟. **We lift them up to the Lord.**

℣. **Let us give thanks to the Lord our God.**
℟. **It is right to give him thanks and praise.**

Father, all-powerful and ever-living God,
we do well always and everywhere to give you thanks
for the many wonders of love and grace
poured out upon the Blessed Virgin Mary
by your loving kindness.

You kept her untouched
by the stain of original sin
and the corruption of the grave.
Spotless in her virginity,
she became the fitting shrine
from which Christ was born
to be revealed as the light of the nations
and the Bridegroom of the Church.
Bathed in the glory of her Son,
she shines upon his people
as a star of hope and a pillar of faith.

In our unending joy we echo on earth
the song of the angels in heaven
as they praise your glory for ever:

Holy, holy, holy Lord, God of power and might,
heaven and earth are full of your glory.
Hosanna in the highest.
Blessed is he who comes in the name of the Lord.
Hosanna in the highest.

MARY, MOTHER OF FAIREST LOVE

P 36

Mary is all-beautiful

℣. **The Lord be with you.**
℟. **And also with you.**

℣. **Lift up your hearts.**
℟. **We lift them up to the Lord.**

℣. **Let us give thanks to the Lord our God.**
℟. **It is right to give him thanks and praise.**

Father, all-powerful and ever-living God,
we do well always and everywhere to give you thanks
and, as we celebrate the memory of the Blessed Virgin Mary,
to proclaim with fitting praise
the greatness of your name.

Beauty was hers at her conception:
free from all stain of sin,
she is resplendent in the glory of grace.

Beauty was hers in her virginal motherhood:
she brought forth her Son, the radiance of your glory,
as the Savior and brother of us all.

Beauty was hers in the passion of her Son:
marked by his blood,
in her meekness she shared the suffering
of the Lamb of God, her Son, silent before his executioners,
and won for herself a new title of motherhood.

Beauty was hers in the resurrection of Christ:
she reigns with him in glory,
the sharer now in his triumph.

Through him the angels of heaven
offer their prayer of adoration
as they rejoice in your presence for ever.
May our voices be one with theirs
in their triumphant hymn of praise:

Holy, holy, holy Lord, God of power and might . . .

MARY, MOTHER OF DIVINE HOPE

P 37

Mary is an example of hope in God

℣. **The Lord be with you.**
℟. **And also with you.**

℣. **Lift up your hearts.**
℟. **We lift them up to the Lord.**

℣. **Let us give thanks to the Lord our God.**
℟. **It is right to give him thanks and praise.**

Father, all-powerful and ever-living God,
we do well always and everywhere to give you thanks
with all our hearts
for your gift to our human family
of Jesus Christ, the author of our salvation,
and of Mary, his mother, the model of divine hope.

Your lowly handmaid
placed all her trust in you:
she awaited in hope
and conceived in faith the Son of Man,
whom the prophets had foretold.
With untiring love
she gave herself to his service
and became the mother of all the living.
Mary, the fairest fruit of Christ's redeeming love,
is a sister to all the children of Adam
as they journey toward the fullness of freedom
and raise their eyes to her,
the sign of sure hope and comfort,
until the day of the Lord dawns in glory.

In our joy we sing
with all the choirs of angels:

Holy, holy, holy Lord, God of power and might . . .

MARY, MOTHER OF UNITY **P 38**

The role of the Blessed Virgin in fostering the unity of the Church

℣. **The Lord be with you.**
℟. **And also with you.**

℣. **Lift up your hearts.**
℟. **We lift them up to the Lord.**

℣. **Let us give thanks to the Lord our God.**
℟. **It is right to give him thanks and praise.**

Father, all-powerful and ever-living God,
we do well always and everywhere to give you thanks
through Jesus Christ our Lord.

He is the one who makes whole,
the lover of unity,
who chose for his mother
a woman unstained in heart and body,
and for his Bride
the one and undivided Church.

Lifted high above the earth,
in the presence of his mother,
he gathered your scattered children into unity,
joining them to himself
with bonds of love.

Returning to you
and seated at your right hand,
he sent upon the Blessed Virgin,
at prayer with the apostles,
the Spirit of concord and unity,
of peace and forgiveness.

We praise you, Lord,
with all the angels and saints in their song of joy:

Holy, holy, holy Lord, God of power and might . . .

MARY, QUEEN AND MOTHER OF MERCY P 39

The Blessed Virgin is queen of pity and mother of mercy

℣. **The Lord be with you.**
℟. **And also with you.**

℣. **Lift up your hearts.**
℟. **We lift them up to the Lord.**

℣. **Let us give thanks to the Lord our God.**
℟. **It is right to give him thanks and praise.**

**Father, all-powerful and ever-living God,
we do well always and everywhere to give you thanks,
and, as we celebrate the memory of the Blessed Virgin Mary,
to proclaim with fitting praise
the greatness of your name.**

**She is the gracious queen
who has herself uniquely known your loving kindness
and stretches out her arms
to embrace all who take refuge in her
and call upon her help in their distress.**

**She is the mother of mercy,
always attentive to the voice of her children,
seeking to win your compassion for them,
and asking your forgiveness for their sins.**

**She is the handmaid of your love,
never ceasing to pray for us to your Son,
that he may enrich our poverty with his grace
and strengthen our weakness with his power.**

**Through him the angels of heaven
offer their prayer of adoration
as they rejoice in your presence for ever.
May our voices be one with theirs
in their triumphant hymn of praise:**

Holy, holy, holy Lord, God of power and might . . .

MARY, MOTHER OF DIVINE PROVIDENCE **P 40**

The Blessed Virgin is the handmaid of God's love and a generous mother to her children

℣. **The Lord be with you.**
℟. **And also with you.**

℣. **Lift up your hearts.**
℟. **We lift them up to the Lord.**

℣. **Let us give thanks to the Lord our God.**
℟. **It is right to give him thanks and praise.**

**Father, all-powerful and ever-living God,
we do well always and everywhere to give you thanks
through Jesus Christ our Lord.**

**In the wisdom of your providence
the Blessed Virgin Mary was overshadowed by the Holy Spirit
and gave birth to the Savior of the world.**

**In Cana of Galilee,
when she interceded with her Son
for the bridegroom and bride,
he gave the first of his signs:
water was turned into wine,
the wedding guests rejoiced,
and the disciples believed in their Master.**

**Now, enthroned as queen at her Son's right hand,
she provides for all the needs of the Church
as the handmaid of your love
and as a mother who cares for each of her children,
entrusted to her by Christ Jesus
while he hung upon the cross.**

**Now with all the saints and angels,
we praise you for ever:**

Holy, holy, holy Lord, God of power and might . . .

MARY, MOTHER OF CONSOLATION **P 41**

The Blessed Virgin, consoled by the Lord, in her turn consoles her children

℣. **The Lord be with you.**
℟. **And also with you.**

℣. **Lift up your hearts.**
℟. **We lift them up to the Lord.**

℣. **Let us give thanks to the Lord our God.**
℟. **It is right to give him thanks and praise.**

**Father, all-powerful and ever-living God,
we do well always to give you thanks
and to bless and praise you
through Jesus Christ our Lord.**

**He was received with joy by the Blessed Virgin
and brought to birth from her chaste womb
as the consolation of the world.**

**As she endured her bitter agony
at the cross of her Son,
she was consoled by you
with the hope of his resurrection.**

**In company with the apostles
she earnestly prayed and awaited with trust
the coming of the Spirit of consolation and peace.**

**Now, assumed into heaven,
she consoles with a mother's love
all who turn to her with faith,
until the day of the Lord dawns in glory.**

**Now with all the saints and angels,
we praise you for ever:**

Holy, holy, holy Lord, God of power and might . . .

MARY, HELP OF CHRISTIANS P 42

The Blessed Virgin as the mother and help of Christians

℣. **The Lord be with you.**
℟. **And also with you.**

℣. **Lift up your hearts.**
℟. **We lift them up to the Lord.**

℣. **Let us give thanks to the Lord our God.**
℟. **It is right to give him thanks and praise.**

**Father, all-powerful and ever-living God,
we do well always and everywhere to give you thanks
through Jesus Christ our Lord.**

**You chose the immaculate Virgin Mary,
the mother of your Son,
to be the mother and help of Christians,
so that under her protection
we might be fearless in waging the battle of faith,
steadfast in holding the teaching of the apostles,
and tranquil in spirit in the storms of this world,
until we reach the joy of your heavenly city.**

**With steadfast love
we sing your unending praise;
we join with the hosts of heaven
in their triumphant song:**

**Holy, holy, holy Lord, God of power and might,
heaven and earth are full of your glory.
Hosanna in the highest.
Blessed is he who comes in the name of the Lord.
Hosanna in the highest.**

OUR LADY OF RANSOM

P 43

Holy Mary as mother of the Redeemer and handmaid of redemption

℣. **The Lord be with you.**
℟. **And also with you.**

℣. **Lift up your hearts.**
℟. **We lift them up to the Lord.**

℣. **Let us give thanks to the Lord our God.**
℟. **It is right to give him thanks and praise.**

**Father, all-powerful and ever-living God,
we do well always and everywhere to give you thanks.**

**In your wise and provident plan
you joined the Blessed Virgin
so closely to your Son
in the work of redemption
that she was with him
as a loving mother in his infancy,
stood by his cross
as the faithful companion in his passion,
and, assumed into heaven,
became our advocate,
and the handmaid of our redemption.**

**She cares unceasingly with a mother's love
for all your children in their need,
breaking the chains of every form of captivity,
that they might enjoy full liberty of body and spirit.**

**Now, with the angels and all the saints
we praise the redeeming love of your Son
and through him we proclaim your greatness,
as we cry out with one voice:**

Holy, holy, holy Lord, God of power and might . . .

MARY, HEALTH OF THE SICK **P 44**

The Blessed Virgin is a sign of salvation for the sick

℣. **The Lord be with you.**
℟. **And also with you.**

℣. **Lift up your hearts.**
℟. **We lift them up to the Lord.**

℣. **Let us give thanks to the Lord our God.**
℟. **It is right to give him thanks and praise.**

Father, all-powerful and ever-living God,
we do well always and everywhere to give you thanks.

In a wonderful way you gave the Blessed Virgin Mary
a special share in the mystery of pain.
She now shines radiantly
as a sign of health, of healing, and of divine hope
for the sick who call on her patronage.
To all who look up to her in prayer
she is the model of perfect acceptance of your will
and of wholehearted conformity with Christ,
who, out of love for us,
endured our weakness
and bore our sufferings.

Through Christ the angels of heaven
offer their prayer of adoration
as they rejoice in your presence for ever.
May our voices be one with theirs
in their triumphant hymn of praise:

Holy, holy, holy Lord, God of power and might,
heaven and earth are full of your glory.
  Hosanna in the highest.
Blessed is he who comes in the name of the Lord.
  Hosanna in the highest.

MARY, QUEEN OF PEACE

P 45

The Mother of Christ is daughter and queen of peace

℣. **The Lord be with you.**
℟. **And also with you.**

℣. **Lift up your hearts.**
℟. **We lift them up to the Lord.**

℣. **Let us give thanks to the Lord our God.**
℟. **It is right to give him thanks and praise.**

Father, all-powerful and ever-living God,
we do well always and everywhere to give you thanks
and, as we honor the memory of the Blessed Virgin Mary,
to proclaim with fitting praise
the greatness of your name.

She is your lowly handmaid,
receiving your word from the angel Gabriel
and conceiving in her virginal womb
the Prince of Peace, Jesus Christ,
your Son, our Lord.

She is the faithful mother,
standing fearless beside the cross
as her Son sheds his blood for our salvation
and reconciles all things to himself in peace.

She is the disciple of Christ and daughter of peace,
joining in prayer with the apostles
as she awaits your promised Gift,
the Spirit of unity and peace, of love and joy.

Now, with the saints and all the angels
we praise you for ever:

Holy, holy, holy Lord, God of power and might,
heaven and earth are full of your glory.
  Hosanna in the highest.
Blessed is he who comes in the name of the Lord.
  Hosanna in the highest.

MARY, GATE OF HEAVEN

P 46

The gate closed by Eve has been reopened by the Blessed Virgin

℣. **The Lord be with you.**
℟. **And also with you.**

℣. **Lift up your hearts.**
℟. **We lift them up to the Lord.**

℣. **Let us give thanks to the Lord our God.**
℟. **It is right to give him thanks and praise.**

**Father, all-powerful and ever-living God,
we do well always and everywhere to give you thanks
and to praise and bless your holy name
as we celebrate the memory
of the Blessed Virgin Mary.**

**She is the Virgin Mother,
prefigured in the eastern gate of the temple,
through which the Lord would enter,
and after him no other.**

**She is the humble Virgin,
whose faith opened the gate of eternal life,
closed by the disbelief of Eve.**

**She is the Virgin at prayer,
always interceding for sinners
that they may turn to her Son,
who unseals the fountain of ever-flowing grace
and opens the door of forgiveness.**

**Through him the angels of heaven
offer their prayer of adoration
as they rejoice in your presence for ever.
May our voices be one with theirs
in their triumphant hymn of praise:**

Holy, holy, holy Lord, God of power and might . . .

BLESSED VIRGIN MARY I

P 47

Motherhood of Mary

℣. **The Lord be with you.**
℟. **And also with you.**

℣. **Lift up your hearts.**
℟. **We lift them up to the Lord.**

℣. **Let us give thanks to the Lord our God.**
℟. **It is right to give him thanks and praise.**

Father, all-powerful and ever-living God,
we do well always and everywhere to give you thanks
(as we celebrate . . . of the Blessed Virgin Mary).
(as we honor the Blessed Virgin Mary).

Through the power of the Holy Spirit,
she became the virgin mother of your only Son,
our Lord Jesus Christ,
who is for ever the light of the world.

Through him the choirs of angels
and all the powers of heaven
praise and worship your glory.
May our voices blend with theirs
as we join in their unending hymn:

Holy, holy, holy Lord, God of power and might,
heaven and earth are full of your glory.
Hosanna in the highest.
Blessed is he who comes in the name of the Lord.
Hosanna in the highest.

BLESSED VIRGIN MARY II

P 48

The Church echoes Mary's song of praise

℣. **The Lord be with you.**
℟. **And also with you.**

℣. **Lift up your hearts.**
℟. **We lift them up to the Lord.**

℣. **Let us give thanks to the Lord our God.**
℟. **It is right to give him thanks and praise.**

**Father, all-powerful and ever-living God,
we do well always and everywhere to give you thanks,
and to praise you for your gifts
as we contemplate your saints in glory.**

**In celebrating the memory of the Blessed Virgin Mary,
it is our special joy to echo her song of thanksgiving.
What wonders you have worked throughout the world.
All generations have shared the greatness of your love.
When you looked on Mary your lowly servant,
you raised her to be the mother of Jesus Christ, your Son, our Lord,
the savior of all humankind.**

**Through him the angels of heaven
offer their prayer of adoration
as they rejoice in your presence for ever.
May our voices be one with theirs
in their triumphant hymn of praise:**

**Holy, holy, holy Lord, God of power and might,
heaven and earth are full of your glory.
  Hosanna in the highest.
Blessed is he who comes in the name of the Lord.
  Hosanna in the highest.**

IMMACULATE CONCEPTION

P 49

The mystery of Mary and the Church

℣. **The Lord be with you.**
℟. **And also with you.**

℣. **Lift up your hearts.**
℟. **We lift them up to the Lord.**

℣. **Let us give thanks to the Lord our God.**
℟. **It is right to give him thanks and praise.**

Father, all-powerful and ever-living God,
we do well always and everywhere to give you thanks.

You allowed no stain of Adam's sin
to touch the Virgin Mary.
Full of grace, she was to be a worthy mother of your Son,
your sign of favor to the Church at its beginning,
and the promise of its perfection as the bride of Christ, radiant in beauty.

Purest of virgins, she was to bring forth your Son,
the innocent lamb who takes away our sins.
You chose her from all women to be our advocate with you
and our pattern of holiness.

In our joy we sing to your glory
with all the choirs of angels:

Holy, holy, holy Lord, God of power and might,
heaven and earth are full of your glory.
Hosanna in the highest.
Blessed is he who comes in the name of the Lord.
Hosanna in the highest.

ASSUMPTION

P 50

Mary assumed into glory

℣. **The Lord be with you.**
℟. **And also with you.**

℣. **Lift up your hearts.**
℟. **We lift them up to the Lord.**

℣. **Let us give thanks to the Lord our God.**
℟. **It is right to give him thanks and praise.**

Father, all-powerful and ever-living God,
we do well always and everywhere to give you thanks
through Jesus Christ our Lord.

Today the virgin Mother of God was taken up into heaven
to be the beginning and the pattern of the Church in its perfection,
and a sign of hope and comfort for your people on their pilgrim way.
You would not allow decay to touch her body,
for she had given birth to your Son, the Lord of all life,
in the glory of the incarnation.

In our joy we sing to your glory
with all the choirs of angels:

Holy, holy, holy Lord, God of power and might,
heaven and earth are full of your glory.
Hosanna in the highest.
Blessed is he who comes in the name of the Lord.
Hosanna in the highest.

EUCHARISTIC PRAYER I
ROMAN CANON

In the first eucharistic prayer the words in brackets may be omitted.

Celebrant alone

The priest, with hands extended, says:

**We come to you, Father,
with praise and thanksgiving,
through Jesus Christ your Son.**

He joins his hands and, making the sign of the cross once over both bread and chalice, says:

**Through him we ask you to accept
and bless ✠
these gifts we offer you in sacrifice.**

With hands extended, he continues:

**We offer them for your holy catholic Church,
watch over it, Lord, and guide it;
grant it peace and unity throughout
the world.**

When several are to be named, a general form is used: for N. our bishop and his assistant bishops (General Instruction, no. 172).

**We offer them for N. our Pope,
for N. our bishop,
and for all who hold and teach the catholic
faith
that comes to us from the apostles.**

Commemoration of the living.

Celebrant alone or one of the concelebrants

**Remember, Lord, your people,
especially those for whom we now pray,
N. and N.**

He prays for them briefly with hands joined. Then, with hands extended, he continues:

Remember all of us gathered here before you.
You know how firmly we believe in you
and dedicate ourselves to you.
We offer you this sacrifice of praise
for ourselves and those who are dear to us.
We pray to you, our living and true God,
for our well-being and redemption.

Special forms on pages 169–170.

In union with the whole Church
we honor Mary,
the ever-virgin mother of Jesus Christ our Lord and God.
† **We honor Joseph, her husband,**
the apostles and martyrs
Peter and Paul, Andrew,

[James, John, Thomas, James, Philip,
Bartholomew, Matthew, Simon and Jude;
we honor Linus, Cletus, Clement, Sixtus,
Cornelius, Cyprian, Lawrence, Chrysogonus,
John and Paul, Cosmas and Damian]

and all the saints.
May their merits and prayers
gain us your constant help and protection.

[Through Christ our Lord. Amen.]

SPECIAL FORM of
In union with the whole Church *(Communicantes)*

Christmas and during the octave

In union with the whole Church
we celebrate that day (night)
when Mary without loss of her virginity
gave the world its Savior.
We honor Mary,
the ever-virgin mother of Jesus Christ our Lord
and God. †

Epiphany

In union with the whole Church
we celebrate that day
when your only Son,
sharing your eternal glory,
showed himself in a human body.
We honor Mary,
the ever-virgin mother of Jesus Christ our Lord
and God. †

Holy Thursday

In union with the whole Church
we celebrate that day
when Jesus Christ, our Lord,
was betrayed for us.
We honor Mary,
the ever-virgin mother of Jesus Christ our Lord
and God. †

From the Easter Vigil to the Second Sunday of Easter inclusive

In union with the whole Church
we celebrate that day (night)
when Jesus Christ, our Lord,
rose from the dead in his human body.
We honor Mary,
the ever-virgin mother of Jesus Christ our Lord
and God. †

Ascension

In union with the whole Church
we celebrate that day
when your only Son, our Lord,
took his place with you
and raised our frail human nature to glory.
We honor Mary,
the ever-virgin mother of Jesus Christ our Lord
and God. †

Pentecost

In union with the whole Church
we celebrate the day of Pentecost
when the Holy Spirit appeared to the apostles
in the form of countless tongues.
We honor Mary,
the ever-virgin mother of Jesus Christ our Lord and God. †

SPECIAL FORM of
Father, accept this offering *(Hanc igitur)*

Holy Thursday

Father, accept this offering
from your whole family
in memory of the day when Jesus Christ, our Lord,
gave the mysteries of his body and blood
for his disciples to celebrate.
Grant us your peace in this life,
save us from final damnation,
and count us among those you have chosen.

[Through Christ our Lord. Amen.]

Bless and approve our offering;
make it acceptable to you,
an offering in spirit and in truth.
Let it become for us
the body and blood of Jesus Christ,
your only Son, our Lord.

The day before he suffered
to save us and all men,
that is today,
he took bread in his sacred hands . . .

From the Easter Vigil to the Second Sunday of Easter inclusive

Father, accept this offering
from your whole family
and from those born into the new life
of water and the Holy Spirit,
with all their sins forgiven.
Grant us your peace in this life,
save us from final damnation,
and count us among those you have chosen.

He joins his hands.

[Through Christ our Lord. Amen.]

Celebrant alone

With hands extended, he continues:

Father, accept this offering
from your whole family.
Grant us your peace in this life,
save us from final damnation,
and count us among those you have chosen.

He joins his hands.

[Through Christ our Lord. Amen.]

Celebrant and concelebrants

With hands outstretched over the offerings, he says:

Bless and approve our offering;
make it acceptable to you,
an offering in spirit and in truth.
Let it become for us
the body and blood of Jesus Christ,
your only Son, our Lord.

He joins his hands.

[Through Christ our Lord. Amen.]

The words of the Lord in the following formulas should be spoken clearly and distinctly, as their meaning demands.

The day before he suffered

He takes the bread and, raising it a little above the altar, continues:

he took the bread in his sacred hands

He looks upward.

and looking up to heaven,
to you, his almighty Father,
he gave you thanks and praise.
He broke the bread,
gave it to his disciples, and said:

He bows slightly.

Take this, all of you, and eat it:
this is my body which will be given up for you.

He shows the consecrated host to the people, places it on the paten, and genuflects in adoration.

Then he continues:

When supper was ended,

He takes the chalice, and, raising it a little above the altar, continues:

he took the cup.
Again he gave you thanks and praise,
gave the cup to his disciples, and said:

He bows slightly.

Take this, all of you, and drink from it:
this is the cup of my blood,
the blood of the new and everlasting covenant.
It will be shed for you and for all
so that sins may be forgiven.
Do this in memory of me.

He shows the chalice to the people, places it on the corporal, and genuflects in adoration.

Celebrant alone

Then he sings or says:

Let us proclaim the mystery of faith:

People with celebrant and concelebrants

a **Christ has died,**
Christ is risen,
Christ will come again.

b **Dying you destroyed our death,**
rising you restored our life.
Lord Jesus, come in glory.

c When we eat this bread and drink this cup,
we proclaim your death, Lord Jesus,
until you come in glory.

d Lord, by your cross and resurrection
you have set us free.
You are the Savior of the world.

Celebrant and concelebrants

Then with hands extended, the priest says:

Father, we celebrate the memory of Christ, your Son.
We, your people and your ministers,
recall his passion,
his resurrection from the dead,
and his ascension into glory;
and from the many gifts you have given us
we offer to you, God of glory and majesty,
this holy and perfect sacrifice:
the bread of life
and the cup of eternal salvation.

Look with favor on these offerings
and accept them as once you accepted
the gifts of your servant Abel,
the sacrifice of Abraham, our father in faith,
and the bread and wine offered by your priest Melchisedech.

Bowing, with hands joined, he continues:

Almighty God,
we pray that your angel may take this sacrifice
to your altar in heaven.
Then, as we receive from this altar

He stands up straight and makes the sign of the cross, saying:

the sacred body and blood of your Son,
let us be filled with every grace and blessing.

He joins his hands.

[Through Christ our Lord. Amen.]

Commemoration of the dead.

Celebrant alone or one of the concelebrants

With hands extended, he says:

Remember, Lord, those who have died
and have gone before us marked with the sign of faith,
especially those for whom we now pray, N. and N.

The priest prays for them briefly with joined hands. Then, with hands extended, he continues:

May these, and all who sleep in Christ,
find in your presence
light, happiness, and peace.

He joins his hands.

[Through Christ our Lord. Amen.]

With hands extended, he continues:

For ourselves, too, we ask
some share in the fellowship of your apostles and martyrs,
with John the Baptist, Stephen, Matthias, Barnabas,
[Ignatius, Alexander, Marcellinus, Peter,
Felicity, Perpetua, Agatha, Lucy,
Agnes, Cecilia, Anastasia]
and all the saints.

The priest strikes his breast with the right hand, saying:

Though we are sinners,
we trust in your mercy and love.

With hands extended as before, he continues:

Do not consider what we truly deserve,
but grant us your forgiveness.

He joins his hands.

Through Christ our Lord.

Celebrant alone

He continues:

Through him you give us all these gifts.
You fill them with life and goodness,
you bless them and make them holy.

Celebrant alone or with the concelebrants

He takes the chalice and the paten with the host and, lifting them up, sings or says:

Through him,
with him,
in him,
in the unity of the Holy Spirit,
all glory and honor is yours,
almighty Father,
for ever and ever.

The people respond: **Amen.**

EUCHARISTIC PRAYER II

Priest: **The Lord be with you.**
People: **And also with you.**

Priest: **Lift up your hearts.**
People: **We lift them up to the Lord.**

Priest: **Let us give thanks to the Lord our God.**
People: **It is right to give him thanks and praise.**

Celebrant alone

**Father, it is our duty and our salvation,
always and everywhere
to give you thanks
through your beloved Son, Jesus Christ.**

**He is the Word through whom you made
the universe,
the Savior you sent to redeem us.
By the power of the Holy Spirit
he took flesh and was born of the Virgin
Mary.**

**For our sake he opened his arms on
the cross;
he put an end to death
and revealed the resurrection.
In this he fulfilled your will
and won for you a holy people.**

**And so we join the angels and the saints
in proclaiming your glory
as we say:**

Holy, Holy, holy Lord, God of power and might,
heaven and earth are full of your glory.
Hosanna in the highest.
Blessed is he who comes in the name of the Lord.
Hosanna in the highest.

Celebrant alone

The priest, with hands extended, says:

Lord, you are holy indeed,
the fountain of all holiness.

Celebrant and concelebrants

He joins his hands and holding them outstretched over the offerings, says:

Let your Spirit come upon these gifts to make them holy,

He joins his hands, and making the sign of the cross once over both bread and chalice, says:

so that they may become for us
the body ✠ and blood of our Lord, Jesus Christ.

He joins his hands.

The words of the Lord in the following formulas should be spoken clearly and distinctly, as their meaning demands.

Before he was given up to death,
a death he freely accepted,

He takes the bread and, raising it a little above the altar, continues:

he took the bread and gave you thanks.
He broke the bread,
gave it to his disciples, and said:

He bows slightly.

Take this, all of you, and eat it:
this is my body which will be given up for you.

He shows the consecrated host to the people, places it on the paten, and genuflects in adoration.

Then he continues:

When supper was ended, he took the cup.

He takes the chalice and, raising it a little above the altar, continues:

**Again he gave you thanks and praise,
gave the cup to his disciples, and said:**

He bows slightly.

**Take this, all of you, and drink from it:
this is the cup of my blood,
the blood of the new and everlasting
covenant.
It will be shed for you and for all
so that sins may be forgiven.
Do this in memory of me.**

He shows the chalice to the people, places it on the corporal and genuflects in adoration.

Celebrant alone

Then he sings or says:

Let us proclaim the mystery of faith:

People with celebrant and concelebrants

a **Christ has died,
Christ is risen,
Christ will come again.**

b **Dying you destroyed our death,
rising you restored our life.
Lord Jesus, come in glory.**

c **When we eat this bread and drink this cup,**
we proclaim your death, Lord Jesus,
until you come in glory.

d **Lord, by your cross and resurrection**
you have set us free.
You are the Savior of the world.

Celebrants and concelebrants

Then, with hands extended, the priest says:

In memory of his death and resurrection,
we offer you, Father, this life-giving bread,
this saving cup.
We thank you for counting us worthy
to stand in your presence and serve you.
May all of us who share in the body and blood of Christ
be brought together in unity by the Holy Spirit.

Celebrant alone or one of the concelebrants

Lord, remember your Church throughout the world;
make us grow in love,
together with N. **our Pope,**
N. **our bishop, and all the clergy.**

When several are to be named, a general form is used: for N. our bishop and his assistant bishops (General Instruction, no. 172).

In Masses for the dead the following may be added:

Remember N.**, whom you have called from this life.**
In baptism he (she) **died with Christ:**
may he (she) **also share his resurrection.**

Remember our brothers and sisters
who have gone to their rest
in the hope of rising again;
bring them and all the departed
into the light of your presence.
Have mercy on us all;
make us worthy to share eternal life
with Mary, the virgin Mother of God,
with the apostles, and with all the saints
who have done your will throughout
the ages.
May we praise you in union with them,
and give you glory,

He joins his hands.

through your Son, Jesus Christ.

Celebrant alone or with the concelebrants

He takes the chalice and the paten with the host and, lifting them up, sings or says:

Through him,
with him,
in him,
in the unity of the Holy Spirit,
all glory and honor is yours,
almighty Father,
for ever and ever.

The people respond: **Amen.**

EUCHARISTIC PRAYER III

Celebrant alone

The priest, with hands extended, says:

**Father, you are holy indeed,
and all creation rightly gives you praise.
All life, all holiness comes from you
through your Son, Jesus Christ our Lord,
by the working of the Holy Spirit.
From age to age you gather a people to
yourself,
so that from east to west
a perfect offering may be made
to the glory of your name.**

Celebrant and concelebrants

He joins his hands and, holding them outstretched over the offerings, says:

**And so, Father, we bring you these gifts.
We ask you to make them holy by the power
of your Spirit,**

He joins his hands and, making the sign of the cross once over both bread and chalice, says:

**that they may become the body ✠ and blood
of your Son, our Lord Jesus Christ,
at whose command we celebrate this
eucharist.**

He joins his hands.

The words of the Lord in the following formulas should be spoken clearly and distinctly, as their meaning demands.

On the night he was betrayed,

He takes the bread and, raising it a little above the altar, continues:

he took bread and gave you thanks
and praise.
He broke the bread, gave it to his disciples,
and said:

He bows slightly.

Take this, all of you, and eat it:
this is my body which will be given up
for you.

He shows the consecrated host to the people, places it on the paten, and genuflects in adoration.

Then he continues:

When supper was ended, he took the cup.

He takes the chalice and, raising it a little above the altar, continues:

Again he gave you thanks and praise,
gave the cup to his disciples, and said:

He bows slightly.

Take this, all of you, and drink from it:
this is the cup of my blood,
the blood of the new and everlasting
covenant.
It will be shed for you and for all
so that sins may be forgiven.
Do this in memory of me.

He shows the chalice to the people, places it on the corporal and genuflects in adoration.

Celebrant alone

Then he sings or says: **Let us proclaim the mystery of faith:**

People with celebrant and concelebrants

a **Christ has died,**
Christ is risen,
Christ will come again.

b **Dying you destroyed our death,**
rising you restored our life.
Lord Jesus, come in glory.

c **When we eat this bread and drink this cup,**
we proclaim your death, Lord Jesus,
until you come in glory.

d **Lord, by your cross and resurrection**
you have set us free.
You are the Savior of the world.

Celebrant and concelebrants

With hands extended, the priest says:

Father, calling to mind the death your Son endured for our salvation,
his glorious resurrection and ascension into heaven,
and ready to greet him when he comes again,
we offer you in thanksgiving this holy and living sacrifice.

Look with favor on your Church's offering,
and see the Victim whose death has reconciled us to yourself.
Grant that we, who are nourished by his body and blood,
may be filled with his Holy Spirit,
and become one body, one spirit in Christ.

Celebrant alone or one of the concelebrants

May he make us an everlasting gift to you
and enable us to share in the inheritance of your saints,
with Mary, the virgin Mother of God;
with the apostles, the martyrs,
(Saint N.—the saint of the day or the patron saint) **and all your saints,**
on whose constant intercession we rely for help.

Lord, may this sacrifice,
which has made our peace with you,
advance the peace and salvation of all the world.
Strengthen in faith and love your pilgrim Church on earth;
your servant, Pope N., our bishop N.,
and all the bishops,
with the clergy and the entire people your Son has gained for you.

When several are to be named, a general form is used: for N. our bishop and his assistant bishops (General Instruction, no. 172).

Father, hear the prayers of the family you have gathered here before you.
In mercy and love unite all your children wherever they may be.*

In Masses for the dead, see page 186.

Welcome into your kingdom our departed brothers and sisters,
and all who have left this world in your friendship.

He joins his hands.

We hope to enjoy for ever the vision of your glory,
through Christ our Lord, from whom all good things come.

Celebrant alone or with the concelebrants

He takes the chalice and the paten with the host and, lifting them up, sings or says:

Through him,
with him,
in him,
in the unity of the Holy Spirit,
all glory and honor is yours,
almighty Father,
for ever and ever.

The people respond: **Amen.**

*When this eucharistic prayer is used in Masses for the dead, the following may be said:

Remember N.
In baptism he (she) died with Christ:
may he (she) also share his resurrection,
when Christ will raise our mortal bodies
and make them like his own in glory.

Welcome into your kingdom our departed brothers and sisters,
and all who have left this world in your friendship.
There we hope to share in your glory
when every tear will be wiped away.
On that day we shall see you, our God, as you are.

He joins his hands.

We shall become like you
and praise you for ever through Christ our Lord,
from whom all good things come.

He takes the chalice and the paten with the host and, lifting them up, says:

Through him,
with him,
in him,
in the unity of the Holy Spirit,
all glory and honor is yours,
almighty Father,
for ever and ever.

The people respond: **Amen.**

EUCHARISTIC PRAYER IV

Priest: **The Lord be with you.**
People: **And also with you.**

Priest: **Lift up your hearts.**
People: **We lift them up to the Lord.**

Priest: **Let us give thanks to the Lord our God.**
People: **It is right to give him thanks and praise.**

Celebrant alone

Father in heaven,
it is right that we should give you thanks and glory:
you are the one God, living and true.
Through all eternity you live in unapproachable light.
Source of life and goodness, you have created all things,
to fill your creatures with every blessing
and lead all men to the joyful vision of your light.
Countless hosts of angels stand before you to do your will;
they look upon your splendor
and praise you, night and day.
United with them,
and in the name of every creature under heaven,
we too praise your glory as we say:

Holy, holy, holy Lord, God of power and might,
heaven and earth are full of your glory.
Hosanna in the highest.
Blessed is he who comes in the name of the Lord.
Hosanna in the highest.

Celebrant alone

The priest, with hands extended, says:

**Father, we acknowledge your greatness:
all your actions show your wisdom and love.
You formed man in your own likeness
and set him over the whole world
to serve you, his creator,
and to rule over all creatures.
Even when he disobeyed you and lost your friendship
you did not abandon him to the power of death
but helped all men to seek and find you.
Again and again you offered a covenant to man,
and through the prophets taught him to hope for salvation.
Father, you so loved the world
that in the fullness of time you sent your only Son to be our Savior.
He was conceived through the power of the Holy Spirit,
and born of the Virgin Mary,
a man like us in all things but sin.
To the poor he proclaimed the good news of salvation,
to prisoners, freedom,
and to those in sorrow, joy.
In fulfillment of your will
he gave himself up to death;
but by rising from the dead,
he destroyed death and restored life.
And that we might live no longer for ourselves but for him,
he sent the Holy Spirit from you, Father,
as his first gift to those who believe,
to complete his work on earth
and bring us the fullness of grace.**

Celebrant and concelebrants

He joins his hands and, holding them outstretched over the offerings, says:

Father, may this Holy Spirit sanctify these offerings.

He joins his hands and, making the sign of the cross once over both bread and chalice, says:

Let them become the body ✠ and blood of Jesus Christ our Lord

He joins his hands.

as we celebrate the great mystery
which he left us as an everlasting covenant.

The words of the Lord in the following formulas should be spoken clearly and distinctly, as their meaning demands.

He always loved those who were his own in the world.
When the time came for him to be glorified by you, his heavenly Father,
he showed the depth of his love.

He takes the bread and, raising it a little above the altar, continues:

While they were at supper,
he took the bread, said the blessing, broke the bread
and gave it to his disciples, saying:

He bows slightly.

Take this, all of you, and eat it:
this is my body which will be given up for you.

He shows the consecrated host to the people, places it on the paten, and genuflects in adoration.

Then he continues:

In the same way, he took the cup, filled with wine.

He takes the chalice, and, raising it a little above the altar, continues:

He gave you thanks, and giving the cup to his disciples, said:

He bows slightly.

Take this, all of you, and drink from it:
this is the cup of my blood,
the blood of the new and everlasting covenant.
It will be shed for you and for all
so that sins may be forgiven.
Do this in memory of me.

He shows the chalice to the people, places it on the corporal, and genuflects in adoration.

Celebrant alone

Then he sings or says:

Let us proclaim the mystery of faith:

People with celebrant and concelebrants

a **Christ has died,**
Christ is risen,
Christ will come again.

b **Dying you destroyed our death,**
rising you restored our life.
Lord Jesus, come in glory.

c **When we eat this bread and drink this cup,**
we proclaim your death, Lord Jesus,
until you come in glory.

d **Lord, by your cross and resurrection**
you have set us free.
You are the Savior of the world.

Celebrant and concelebrants

With hands extended, the priest says:

Father, we now celebrate this memorial of our redemption.
We recall Christ's death, his descent among the dead,
his resurrection, and his ascension to your right hand;
and, looking forward to his coming in glory,
we offer you his body and blood,
the acceptable sacrifice
which brings salvation to the whole world.

Lord, look upon this sacrifice which you have given to your Church;
and by your Holy Spirit, gather all who share this one bread and one cup
into the one body of Christ, a living sacrifice of praise.

Celebrant alone or one of the concelebrants

Lord, remember those for whom we offer this sacrifice,
especially N., our Pope,
N. our bishop, and bishops and clergy everywhere.

When several are to be named, a general form is used: for N. our bishop and his assistant bishops (General Instruction, no. 172).

Remember those who take part in this offering,
those here present and all your people,
and all who seek you with a sincere heart.
Remember those who have died in the peace of Christ
and all the dead whose faith is known to you alone.

Father, in your mercy grant also to us, your children,
to enter into our heavenly inheritance
in the company of the Virgin Mary, the Mother of God,
and your apostles and saints.
Then, in your kingdom, freed from the corruption of sin and death,
we shall sing your glory with every creature through Christ our Lord,

He joins his hands.

through whom you give us everything that is good.

Celebrant alone or with the concelebrants

He takes the chalice and the paten with the host and, lifting them up, sings or says:

Through him,
with him,
in him,
in the unity of the Holy Spirit,
all glory and honor is yours,
almighty Father,
for ever and ever.

The people respond:

Amen.

Through him, with him, in him, in the u - ni - ty of the Ho - ly Spir - it, all glo - ry

and hon - or is yours, al - might - y Fa - ther, for ev - er and ev - er. ℟. A - men.

COMMUNION RITE

LORD'S PRAYER
The priest sets down the chalice and paten and with hands joined, sings or says one of the following:

a **Let us pray with confidence to the Father in the words our Savior gave us.**

b **Jesus taught us to call God our Father, and so we have the courage to say:**

c **Let us ask our Father to forgive our sins and to bring us to forgive those who sin against us.**

d **Let us pray for the coming of the kingdom as Jesus taught us.**

He extends his hands and he continues, with the people:

Our Father, who art in heaven,
hallowed be thy name;
thy kingdom come;
thy will be done on earth as it is in heaven.
Give us this day our daily bread;
and forgive us our trespasses
as we forgive those who trespass against us;
and lead us not into temptation,
but deliver us from evil.

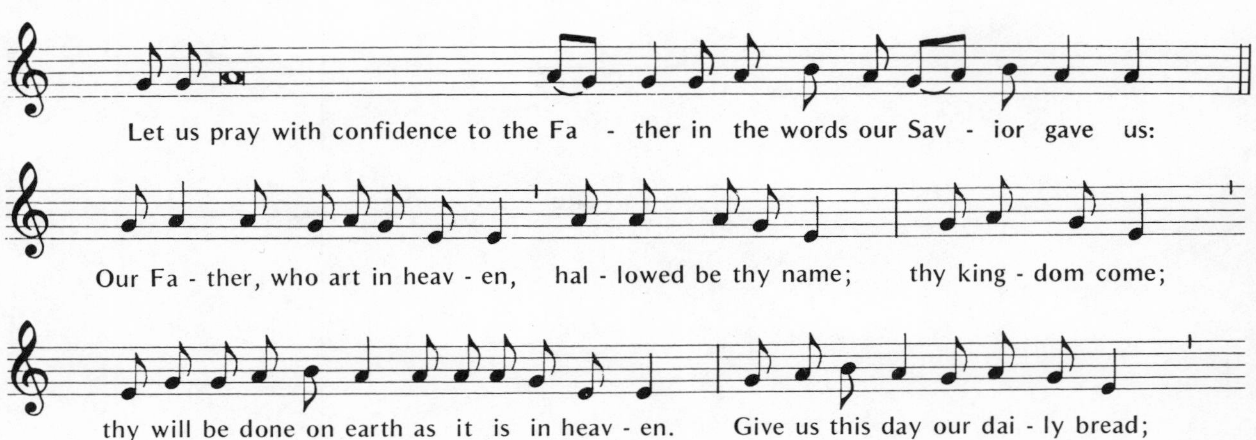

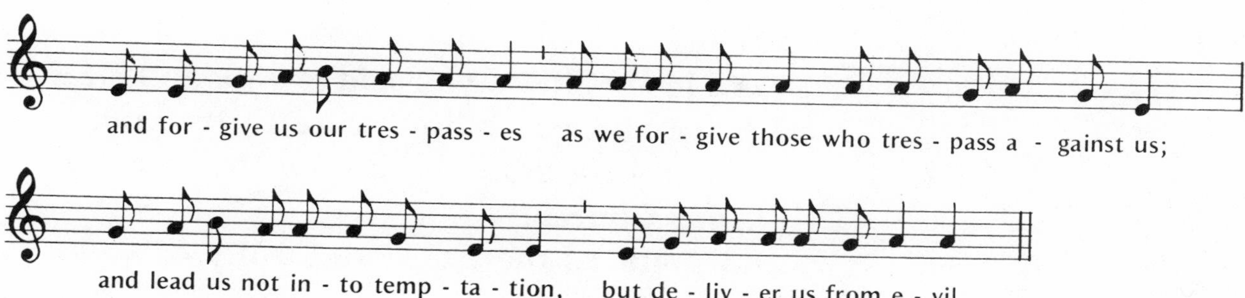

With hands extended, the priest continues alone:

**Deliver us, Lord, from every evil,
and grant us peace in our day.
In your mercy keep us free from sin
and protect us from all anxiety
as we wait in joyful hope
for the coming of our Savior, Jesus Christ.**

He joins his hands.

DOXOLOGY

The people end the prayer with the acclamation:

**For the kingdom, the power, and the glory
are yours, now and for ever.**

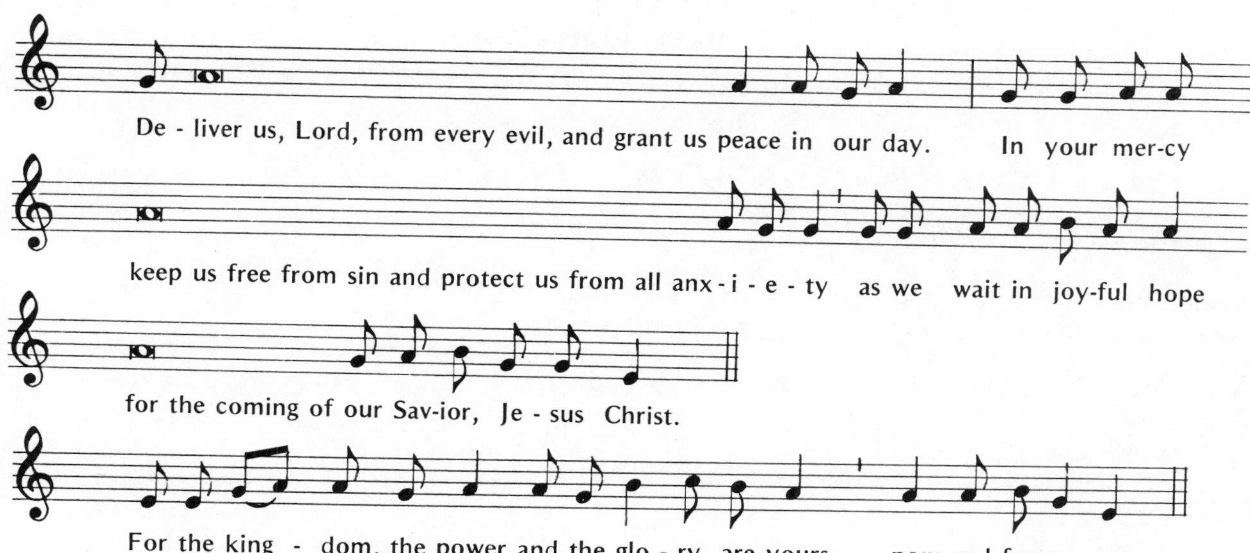

SIGN OF PEACE

Then the priest, with hands extended, says aloud:

Lord Jesus Christ, you said to your apostles:
I leave you peace, my peace I give you.
Look not on our sins, but on the faith of your Church,

He joins his hands.

and grant us the peace and unity of your kingdom
where you live for ever and ever.

The people answer:

Amen.

The priest, extending and joining his hands, adds:

The peace of the Lord by with you always.

The people answer:

And also with you.

Then the deacon (or the priest) may add:

Let us offer each other the sign of peace.

All make an appropriate sign of peace, according to local custom. The priest gives the sign of peace to the deacon or minister.

BREAKING OF THE BREAD

Then the following is sung or said:

Lamb of God, you take away the sins of the world:
have mercy on us.
Lamb of God, you take away the sins of the world:
have mercy on us.
Lamb of God, you take away the sins of the world:
grant us peace.

This may be repeated until the breaking of the bread is finished, but the last phrase is always Grant us peace.

Meanwhile, he takes the host and breaks it over the paten. He places a small piece in the chalice, saying inaudibly:

May this mingling of the body and blood of our Lord Jesus Christ bring eternal life to us who receive it.

Private Preparation of the Priest
(General Instruction, no. 56f)

Then the priest joins his hands and says inaudibly:

a

Lord Jesus Christ, Son of the living God, by the will of the Father and the work of the Holy Spirit your death brought life to the world. By your holy body and blood free me from all my sins and from every evil. Keep me faithful to your teaching, and never let me be parted from you.

b

Lord Jesus Christ, with faith in your love and mercy I eat your body and drink your blood. Let it not bring me condemnation, but health in mind and body.

COMMUNION

The priest genuflects. Taking the host, he raises it slightly over the paten and, facing the people, says aloud:

This is the Lamb of God
who takes away the sins of the world.
Happy are those who are called to
his supper.

He adds, once only, with the people:

Lord, I am not worthy to receive you,
but only say the word and I shall be healed.

Facing the altar, the priest says inaudibly:

May the body of Christ bring me to
everlasting life.

He reverently consumes the body of Christ. Then he takes the chalice and says inaudibly:

May the blood of Christ bring me to
everlasting life.

He reverently drinks the blood of Christ.

After this he takes the paten or other vessel and goes to the communicants. He takes a host for each one, raises it a little, and shows it, saying:

The body of Christ.

The communicant answers:

Amen.

and receives communion.

When a deacon gives communion, he does the same.

The sign of communion is more complete when given under both kinds, since the sign of the eucharistic meal appears more clearly. The intention of Christ that the new and eternal covenant be ratified in his blood is better expressed, as is the relation of the eucharistic banquet to the heavenly banquet (General Instruction, no. 240).

If any are receiving in both kinds, the rite described elsewhere is followed. When he presents the chalice, the priest or deacon says:

The blood of Christ.

The communicant answers:

Amen.

and drinks it.

The deacon and other ministers may receive communion from the chalice (General Instruction, no. 242).

COMMUNION SONG

While the priest receives the body of Christ, the communion song is begun.

The vessels are cleansed by the priest or deacon or acolyte after the communion or after Mass, if possible at the side table (General Instruction, no. 238).

Meanwhile he says inaudibly:

Lord, may I receive these gifts in purity
of heart.
May they bring me healing and strength,
now and for ever.

PERIOD OF SILENCE OR SONG OF PRAISE

Then the priest may return to the chair. A period of silence may now be observed, or a psalm or song of praise may be sung.

PRAYER AFTER COMMUNION

Then, standing at the chair or at the altar, the priest sings or says:

Let us pray.

Priest and people pray in silence for a while, unless a period of silence has already been observed. Then the priest extends his hands and sings or says the prayer after communion, at the end of which the people respond:

Amen.

CONCLUDING RITE

If there are any brief announcements, they are made at this time.

GREETING

The rite of dismissal takes place.

Facing the people, the priest extends his hands and sings or says:

The Lord be with you.

The people answer:

And also with you.

BLESSING

A. Simple form

The priest blesses the people with these words:

May almighty God bless you,
the Father, and the Son, ✠
and the Holy Spirit.

The people answer:

Amen.

On certain days or occasions another more solemn form of blessing or prayer over the people may be used as the rubrics direct.

B. Solemn blessing

Texts of all solemn blessings are given on pages 201–205.

Deacon: **Bow your heads and pray for God's blessing.**

The priest always concludes the solemn blessing by adding:

May almighty God bless you,
the Father, and the Son, ✢
and the Holy Spirit.

The people answer: **Amen.**

DISMISSAL

The dismissal sends each member of the congregation to do good works, praising and blessing the Lord. (See General Instruction, no. 57).

The deacon (or the priest), with hands joined, sings or says:

a Go in the peace of Christ.

b The Mass is ended, go in peace.

c Go in peace to love and serve the Lord.

The people answer: **Thanks be to God.**

The priest kisses the altar as at the beginning. Then he makes the customary reverence with the ministers and leaves.

If any liturgical service follows immediately, the rite of dismissal is omitted.

SOLEMN BLESSINGS

The following blessings may be used at the end of Mass.
The deacon gives the invitation, or in his absence the priest himself may also give it: Bow your heads and pray for God's blessing. Another form of invitation may be used. Then the priest extends his hands over the people while he says the blessing.
All respond: Amen.

ADVENT

**May you be filled with the grace of God the Father,
whose Word was conceived in the womb of the Blessed Virgin
to become the Savior of the human race.**
℟. **Amen.**

**May your hearts never lose the peace of Christ,
whose coming the Blessed Virgin, daughter of Zion,
so joyously awaited.**
℟. **Amen.**

**May the light and grace of the Holy Spirit remain with you,
that you may await the Second Coming of Christ
vigilant in prayer and with songs of praise on your lips.**
℟. **Amen.**

**May almighty God bless you,
the Father, and the Son, ✠ and the Holy Spirit.**
℟. **Amen.**

CHRISTMAS SEASON

**May God, who through the motherhood of the Virgin Mary
dispelled the darkness of ages past,
enlighten your minds with the radiance of the sun of justice.**
℟. **Amen.**

**May God, who sent his Son as the Redeemer of the world,
refashion your minds and hearts in the image of Christ.**
℟. **Amen.**

**Like Mary, mother of Wisdom,
may you gratefully ponder in your hearts
the wonder of God's blessings
and may you find in Christ and the Blessed Virgin
the model of your way of life.**
℟. **Amen.**

**May almighty God bless you,
the Father, and the Son, ✠ and the Holy Spirit.**
℟. **Amen.**

LENT

**Through the sacrifice of Christ,
to which his sorrowful mother united her own loving heart,
God chose to redeem the human race.
May he draw you deeply into that great mystery of salvation.**
℟. **Amen.**

**God led the Blessed Virgin Mary to advance ever further
in faith and in sorrow
until at the foot of the cross she reached the perfection of charity.
May he make your faith ever stronger
and inspire you to love him
with your whole heart and soul and strength.**
℟. **Amen.**

**And when the days of your life are ended,
may you reflect the image of Christ in his passion,
that you may become sharers in his glory.**
℟. **Amen.**

**May almighty God bless you,
the Father, and the Son, ✠ and the Holy Spirit.**
℟. **Amen.**

EASTER SEASON

**God the Father through the resurrection of his Son
gladdened the Blessed Virgin and the infant Church;
may he fill you with every spiritual joy and peace.
℟. Amen.**

**Jesus Christ, who was born of a spotless Virgin,
arose incorruptible from the grave;
may he preserve undiminished in your hearts
the fullness of your baptismal faith.
℟. Amen.**

**May the Holy Spirit,
whose coming the Blessed Virgin, with the apostles,
awaited in sure faith,
dwell with you to purify your hearts.
℟. Amen.**

**May almighty God bless you,
the Father, and the Son, ✠ and the Holy Spirit.
℟. Amen.**

ORDINARY TIME

I

**May the Father of all mercy,
through the love with which he cherished the mother of his Son,
bless you with health of mind and body.
℟. Amen.**

**May Jesus Christ,
the blessed fruit of Mary's womb,
adorn you with the virtues
that will make you more pleasing to him.
℟. Amen.**

**May the Holy Spirit,
whose power overshadowed the Blessed Virgin,
give you serenity and peace,
that you may live as one in mind and heart
in the household of the Church.**
℟. **Amen.**

**May almighty God bless you,
the Father, and the Son, ✠ and the Holy Spirit.**
℟. **Amen.**

II

**May God, who through the motherhood of the Virgin Mary
graciously redeemed the human race,
enrich you with his blessing.**
℟. **Amen.**

**Through Mary you have received the author of life.
May you experience her loving protection
now and at every hour.**
℟. **Amen.**

**You have gathered to celebrate this memorial of our Lady.
May you go forth from here
rejoicing in the spirit and the gifts of heaven.**
℟. **Amen.**

**May almighty God bless you,
the Father, and the Son, ✠ and the Holy Spirit.**
℟. **Amen.**

III

May the Father of mercies bless you
through the intercession of blessed Mary, ever virgin,
through whom he chose to remedy the fall of our first parents.
℟. **Amen.**

May Jesus Christ,
who in the womb of the Blessed Virgin
became our brother and our Savior,
free your hearts from every trace of sin.
℟. **Amen.**

May the Holy Spirit
increase in you the grace of true faith and of hope for heaven,
that you may walk in the ways of the Gospel
and so reach your eternal home.
℟. **Amen.**

May almighty God bless you,
the Father, and the Son, ✠ and the Holy Spirit.
℟. **Amen.**

ORDINARY TIME

During Ordinary Time memorials of the Blessed Virgin occur frequently both in the General Roman Calendar and in the calendars of the particular Churches and of religious institutes. There are consequently a great number of Marian Mass formularies in propers of the Roman rite, which have one and the same object—the work God has accomplished in Mary in relationship to Christ and the Church—but which celebrate it under its many different aspects.

In view of the mystery that they celebrate the Mass formularies for Ordinary Time are divided into three sections. The first section contains eleven formularies to celebrate memorials of the Mother of God under titles that are derived chiefly from Sacred Scripture or that express Mary's bond with the Church. The second section contains nine formularies to celebrate memorials of the Blessed Virgin Mary under titles that refer to her cooperation in fostering the spiritual life of the faithful. The third section contains eight formularies to celebrate memorials of the Blessed Virgin under titles that suggest her compassionate intercession on behalf of the faithful (see *Collection of Masses of the Blessed Virgin Mary,* Introduction, no. 24).

Section 1

This section contains eleven Mass formularies for the celebration of a memorial of the Mother of God under titles that are chiefly derived from Scripture or that bring out Mary's bond with the Church.

19. HOLY MARY, MOTHER OF THE LORD

Among the titles given to the Blessed Virgin in the gospels that of "Mother of the Lord" has a special place. Elizabeth, the mother of Christ's herald, filled with the Holy Spirit (see Luke 1:41), used this title in greeting our Lady: "Why should I be honored with a visit from the mother of my Lord?" (Luke 1:42).

Under the title of "Holy Mary, Mother of the Lord," the formulary provided here is the Mass found in *The Roman Missal (Sacramentary),* Common of the Blessed Virgin Mary, Ordinary Time, no. 3 (MR, pp. 672–673), the texts of which are marked by what is known as "Roman sobriety" and by deep devotion to the mother of Jesus. The preface is taken from the *Proprium missarum Societatis Apostolatus Catholici,* Curia Generalis Ordinis, Rome, 1976, p. 11.

In the preface God the Father is glorified on account of the double maternal role he has assigned in his "wisdom and love" to the Blessed Virgin: in relation to his Son ("In the mother of your Son you showed the wonders of your power") and in relation to his people ("she fulfills a mother's role in the household of the Church").

Entrance Antiphon

You have been blessed, O Virgin Mary, above all other women on earth by the Lord, the Most High God, for God has so exalted your name that human lips will never cease to praise you. *See Judith 13:18, 20*

OPENING PRAYER

Lord,
as we honor the glorious memory of the Virgin Mary,
we ask that by the help of her prayers
we too may come to share the fullness of your grace.

Grant this through our Lord Jesus Christ, your Son,
who lives and reigns with you and the Holy Spirit,
one God, for ever and ever.

PRAYER OVER THE GIFTS

Lord,
we bring you our sacrifice of praise
at this celebration in honor of Mary, the mother of your Son.
Grant that through this holy exchange of gifts
we may advance toward everlasting redemption.

We ask this in the name of Jesus the Lord.

PREFACE **P 19** (Page 134)

Communion Antiphon

All generations will call me blessed, for God has looked with favor on his lowly servant. *See Luke 1:48*

PRAYER AFTER COMMUNION

We have received this heavenly sacrament
and now pray, Lord our God,
that we who honor the memory of the Blessed Virgin Mary
may come to share in the eternal banquet.

We ask this through Christ our Lord.

20. HOLY MARY, THE NEW EVE

As early as the second century, especially in the writings of St. Justin (d. c. 163) and St. Irenaeus (d. c. 200), the Blessed Virgin Mary is seen by the Church as the new Eve or the new woman, intimately associated with Christ, the new Adam (see 1 Corinthians 15:45), in the work of salvation. By her faith and obedience she undoes the loss inflicted on the human race by the unbelief and disobedience of the first Eve: "The knot of Eve's disobedience was loosed by Mary's obedience. The bonds fastened by the virgin Eve through disbelief were untied by the virgin Mary through faith" (St. Irenaeus, *Adversus haereses,* 3:22, 4: Sch, no. 34, p. 82).

In this formulary the saving "mystery of the woman"—of Mary and the Church—is commemorated. Mary, as "type of the Church" (see LG, no. 63), is the woman promised in the Proto-Gospel (see Genesis 3:15), greeted by Elizabeth as blessed among all women (see Luke 1:42), from whom the Son of God became truly human (see Galatians 4:4), anticipating the mysterious "hour" of Jesus at the wedding feast at Cana (see John 2:4), fulfilling her role of mother at the foot of the cross (see John 19:26), resplendent in heaven as the woman clothed with the sun and crowned with stars (see Revelation 12:1).

Mary is thus celebrated as:

—*the firstfruits of the new creation:* "you chose the Blessed Virgin, formed by the Holy Spirit, as the firstfruits of the new creation" (OP; see LG, no. 56).

—*the new earth, where, from the moment of her immaculate conception,* "justice dwells" (see Resp).

—*the firstfruits of the new people of God:* "you made her the firstfruits of your new people" (Pref).

—*a disciple of the New Law:* "the first disciple of the New Law" (Pref).

—*a woman given a new heart by God,* in accordance with the prophecy of Ezekiel (see 1:9): "you formed a new heart for the second Eve" (PAC).

—*a woman preparing the new wine for the Church:* "blessed are you, Virgin Mary . . . through you Christ has prepared the new wine for the Church" (Com Ant, B).

—*a faithful virgin:* "we celebrate the memory of the Blessed Virgin Mary and her complete self-giving to the sacrifice of the New Law" (POG).

—*the new Jerusalem,* the holy city, the dwelling-place of God (see 1 Read, Revelation 21:1-5a).

To sum up: Holy Mary, "conceived without stain, enriched by gifts of grace, . . . is indeed the new woman" (Pref), mother and companion of Christ, author of the New Covenant (see Pref).

Entrance Antiphon

A great sign appeared in heaven: a woman clothed with the sun, the moon beneath her feet, and a crown of twelve stars on her head.

Revelation 12:1

OPENING PRAYER

**Lord our God,
you chose the Blessed Virgin,
formed by the Holy Spirit,
as the firstfruits of the new creation;
grant that we may reject the old ways of sin,
embrace wholeheartedly the new life of the Gospel,
and honor faithfully the new commandment of love.**

**We make our prayer through our Lord Jesus Christ,
your Son,
who lives and reigns with you and the Holy Spirit,
one God, for ever and ever.**

PRAYER OVER THE GIFTS

**Lord,
as we celebrate the memory of the Blessed Virgin Mary
and her complete self-giving
to the sacrifice of the New Law,
we offer you these gifts
as a sign of our worship
and ask that by the power of your grace
we may walk all our days
in the new life you have given us.**

We ask this through Christ our Lord.

PREFACE **P 20** (Page 135)

Communion Antiphon

A **Glorious things are told of you, Virgin Mary, for the Almighty has done great things for you.** *See Psalm 87:3; Luke 1:49*

B **Blessed are you, Virgin Mary: through you God has given us the Savior of the world, through you Christ has prepared the new wine for the Church.**

PRAYER AFTER COMMUNION

Lord our God,
in the Blessed Virgin Mary
you formed a new heart for the second Eve;
grant that by the grace of this sacrament
we may be obedient to the inspiration of the Holy Spirit
and grow more and more each day
in the likeness of Christ, the second Adam,
who lives and reigns for ever and ever.

21. THE HOLY NAME OF THE BLESSED VIRGIN MARY

The Roman Missal (Sacramentary) has a votive Mass of the Most Holy Name of Mary (MR, pp. 869–870), of which only the opening prayer is proper. A memorial of the Most Holy Name of the Virgin is celebrated on 12 September in many particular Churches and religious institutes, generally with the same formulary. The present formulary, except for the preface and a few changes, is taken from the *Proprium missarum Societatis Mariae.*

In this Mass God the Father is glorified first of all on account of ''the name of Jesus,'' that is, on account of ''the person of his Son,'' his power and saving mission: ''In no other name is there salvation'' (Pref, see Acts 4:12); ''at his command every knee must bend, in heaven, on earth, and under the earth'' (Pref, see Philippians 2:10).

The Father is then glorified on account of ''the name of Mary,'' that is, on account of the person of Christ's mother and her mission in the history of salvation (see Pref). The name of the Blessed Virgin Mary is celebrated as:

—*a name of honor, for God* ''has so exalted your name that human lips will never cease to praise you,'' as he brought honor to the name of Judith, who is a type of the Blessed Virgin (Ent Ant, see Judith 13:20);

—*a holy name,* for it marks out the woman who was entirely ''full of grace'' (*All,* see Luke 1:28) and found ''favor with God'' (Gos, Luke 1:30) and so conceived and gave birth to the Son of God (see Luke 1:31);

—*a maternal name,* for the Lord Jesus, ''dying on the altar of the cross . . . gave us as our mother the one he had chosen to be his own mother, the Blessed Virgin Mary'' (OP), so that the faithful as they ''call upon the holy name of Mary, (their) mother, . . . may receive strength and comfort in all (their) needs'' (OP);

—*a name responsive to need,* for the faithful on whose lips the name of the Virgin echoes and re-echoes (see Pref) ''turn to her with confidence as their star of hope, call on her as their mother in time of danger, and seek her protection in their hour of need'' (Pref, see OP).

Entrance Antiphon

You have been blessed, O Virgin Mary, above all other women on earth by the Lord, the Most High God, for God has so exalted your name that human lips will never cease to praise you. *See Judith 13:18, 20*

OPENING PRAYER

Lord our God,
when your Son was dying on the altar of the cross,
he gave us as our mother
the one he had chosen to be his own mother,
the Blessed Virgin Mary;
grant that we who call upon the holy name of Mary,
our mother,
with confidence in her protection
may receive strength and comfort in all our needs.

We make our prayer through our Lord Jesus Christ,
your Son,
who lives and reigns with you and the Holy Spirit,
one God, for ever and ever.

PRAYER OVER THE GIFTS

Lord,
look with favor on the gifts we offer
and grant that our hearts may be enlightened
by the Holy Spirit,
so that in imitation of blessed Mary, ever virgin,
we may seek to be faithful to Christ, your Son,
to live only for him,
and to please him in all that we do.

We ask this through Christ our Lord.

PREFACE **P 21** (Page 136)

Communion Antiphon

All generations will call me blessed, for God has looked with favor on his lowly servant. *See Luke 1:48*

PRAYER AFTER COMMUNION

Lord our God,
you have given us new strength
at the table of your word and sacrament;
grant that by the guidance and patronage of blessed Mary
we may turn away
from all that dishonors the name of Christ
and seek only what brings it into good repute.

We ask this through Christ our Lord.

22. HOLY MARY, HANDMAID OF THE LORD

In the gospel according to Luke the Blessed Virgin twice describes herself as "the handmaid of the Lord": when she gives her consent to the message of the angel (see Luke 1:38), and when she proclaims the greatness of the Lord because of "the great things" he has worked in her (see Luke 1:49). To understand fully the meaning and force of her title of "handmaid of the Lord" we must read it in the light of the songs of the "Servant of the Lord" (see Isaiah 42:1- 7; 49:1-9; 50:1-11; 52:1–53:12), and above all in the light of Jesus Christ as the one who fulfills the figure of the "Servant of the Lord": he "did not come to be served, but to serve, and to give his life as a ransom for the many" (Mark 10:45).

The Blessed Virgin is honored liturgically under the title of "handmaid of the Lord" in certain religious institutes, especially in the Congregation of the Passion of Jesus Christ (Passionists). Most of the texts of this Mass are taken from its *Proprium missarum,* General Curia CP, Rome, 1974, pp. 30–31.

This Mass celebrates the merciful plan of salvation by which God chooses the Blessed Virgin, his lowly handmaid, to be mother and partner of Christ (see OP). As the Second Vatican Council teaches, Mary, "the daughter of Adam, in giving her consent to the word of God, became the mother of Jesus. Embracing wholeheartedly the saving will of God and being unhindered by any sin, she devoted herself completely as the handmaid of the Lord to the person and work of her Son. In subordination to him and with him, by the grace of almighty God she served the mystery of redemption" (LG, no. 56).

The Blessed Virgin, the lowly handmaid of the Lord, is therefore addressed as the "servant of your love" (Pref), giving herself completely to God's service (see POG) and to the work of the Son for the salvation of all (see Pref).

The Mass closely follows the teaching of the Gospel in celebrating Mary, the lowly handmaid, as also raised to royal dignity: she who "gave great service to Christ" was given great honor by the Father (see Pref, John 12:26); "she who saw herself as (God's) lowly handmaid was raised up" by God to "reign as queen in glory in the presence" of his Son (Pref). This is well expressed in the *alleluia* verse: "Blessed are you, O Virgin Mary: you declared yourself the handmaid of the Lord, and now, exalted above the choirs of angels, you are acclaimed by the Church as queen of heaven."

Entrance Antiphon

My spirit rejoices in God my Savior, for he has looked with favor on his lowly servant. *Luke 1:47-48*

OPENING PRAYER

**Lord our God,
in your loving plan of redemption
you chose the Blessed Virgin,
your lowly handmaid,
to be the mother and companion of Christ your Son;
grant that by constantly looking up to her
we may give you wholehearted service
in untiring care for the salvation of the world.**

**We make our prayer through our Lord Jesus Christ,
your Son,
who lives and reigns with you and the Holy Spirit,
one God, for ever and ever.**

PRAYER OVER THE GIFTS

**All-holy Father,
on this memorial of the Blessed Virgin Mary,
your obedient and devoted handmaid,
receive our offerings and gifts
and grant that we may present to you ourselves
as a sacrifice pleasing in your sight.**

We ask this through Christ our Lord.

PREFACE **P 22** (Page 137)

Communion Antiphon

Lord God, look upon me and have pity on me; save the child of your handmaid. *Psalm 86:15-16*

PRAYER AFTER COMMUNION

Lord our God,
you have brought us together
to partake of this spiritual food and drink;
we pray that, in faithful imitation of the Blessed Virgin,
we may always seek to be servants of the Church
and so come to know the joys of fidelity to you.

We ask this through Christ our Lord.

23. THE BLESSED VIRGIN MARY, TEMPLE OF THE LORD

The ''mystery of the temple'' was fulfilled in Christ Jesus (see John 2:19-22), in whom ''the whole fullness of the Godhead dwells in bodily form'' (Colossians 2:9). In Scripture the Church too is called a ''holy temple''; ''you are fellow citizens of the saints and members of God's household, built upon the foundation of the apostles and prophets, Christ Jesus himself being the cornerstone, in whom the whole structure grows into *a holy temple* in the Lord'' (Ephesians 2:19-21). Individual Christians are also ''a temple of God'' because God dwells in their hearts: ''Do you not know that you are *God's temple* and that God's Spirit dwells in you? . . . God's temple is holy, and you are that temple'' (1 Corinthians 3:16-17).

In a unique way the Blessed Virgin is herself ''a holy temple'':

—when she conceived the very Son of God in her immaculate womb, she became a true temple of the true God;

—when she cherished the word of God in her heart (see Luke 2:19, 51), loved Christ so ardently, and faithfully kept his word, the Son and the Father came to her and made their home with her, in accordance with the promise of the Lord (see John 14:23).

This Mass therefore celebrates the divine motherhood of our Lady and her holiness of life under this image of ''the temple.''

Our Lady is called ''a holy temple'' built ''with artistry beyond all telling'' by God for the Son (see OP); a ''temple'' of God's glory ''without compare,'' because of her ''obedience of faith and the mystery of the incarnation'' (Pref); a ''temple of holiness and a temple of love for us sinners . . . temple filled with the Holy Spirit'' *(All).*

Other images are also used to draw out the significance of the Blessed Virgin Mary, all more or less equivalent to the idea of the ''temple'': *a tabernacle* within which God dwells, a dwelling that will always stand firm (Com Ant, Psalm 46:5- 6; see Ent Ant, Revelation 21:3); *a house of the Lord,* which God has filled with his presence (see 1 Read, 1 Kings 8:11; Resp, Psalm 84:11); *a house of gold,* ''adorned by the Spirit with every kind of virtue'' (Pref); *a royal palace,* ''resplendent with the presence of the One who is the Truth'' (Pref), dwelt in by the King of kings; *the holy city,* ''rejoicing in its streams of grace'' (Pref, see Psalm 46:5); *the ark of the covenant,* ''enshrining the author of the New Law'' (Pref).

Entrance Antiphon

I heard a great voice from the throne: "Here God lives among the human race! He will dwell with them, and they will be his people, and God will be with them as their God." *Revelation 21:3*

OPENING PRAYER

Lord God,
with artistry beyond all telling
you fashioned a holy temple for your Son
in the virginal womb of Blessed Mary;
grant that, in faithfully safeguarding the grace
of our baptism,
we may worship you in spirit and in truth
and become like Mary a temple of your glory.

We ask this through our Lord Jesus Christ, your Son,
who lives and reigns with you and the Holy Spirit,
one God, for ever and ever.

PRAYER OVER THE GIFTS

Lord,
receive these gifts from our grateful hearts
as we celebrate this memorial of the Blessed Virgin Mary,
from whose life we learn the secret of prayer and praise.
In your goodness grant that like her
we may offer you a sacrifice of holiness
by doing always what is pleasing in your sight.

We ask this through Christ our Lord.

PREFACE **P 23** (Page 138)

Communion Antiphon

Blessed are you, Virgin Mary, holy tabernacle of the Most High: God dwells within you, God's dwelling will always stand firm.

See Psalm 46:5-6

PRAYER AFTER COMMUNION

Lord our God,
you have nourished us with food and drink from heaven;
grant that, like the Blessed Virgin Mary,
we may serve you in holiness of life,
revere your presence in our neighbor,
and with Mary proclaim your greatness
with sincerity of heart.

We ask this through Christ our Lord.

24. THE BLESSED VIRGIN MARY, SEAT OF WISDOM

Beginning with the tenth century we find in Masses of our Lady, mother of the incarnate Wisdom of God, that readings are often from the Wisdom literature (or "sapiential epistles"), especially Sirach and Proverbs (see OLM, 707:5, 6). In these texts the Church, though listening primarily to the voice of eternal Wisdom, hears also the voice of the Blessed Virgin Mary, for in them, according to the common understanding of the medieval writers, the Wisdom of God speaks in a certain sense "in the person of the Virgin."

From the twelfth century, at morning prayer (lauds) and in litanies in honor of our Lady, a number of titles are given her in praise of her close relationship with eternal Wisdom: *"mother of Wisdom," "fountain of Wisdom," "house of Wisdom," "seat of Wisdom,"* the last of which became the most common.

Under this title the Blessed Virgin is honored, even in liturgical celebrations, in particular Churches, in universities, and in religious institutes, especially the Missionaries of the Company of Mary, founded by St. Louis Grignion de Montfort (d. 1716). The Mass formulary given here, except for the preface, is taken from the *Proprium missarum* of the Missionaries of the Company of Mary.

The title "seat of Wisdom" celebrates the maternal role of our Lady, her royal dignity, and her incomparable wisdom and prudence in the things of God:

—*her maternal role,* because through the mystery of the incarnation the Wisdom of the Father is cradled in the arms of his Virgin Mother;

—*her royal dignity,* because the child sitting on Mary's lap is the messianic King, who will be called "Son of the Most High," to whom "the Lord God will give the throne of his father David, and who will reign over the house of Jacob for ever, and whose kingdom will never end" (Luke 1:32-33; see Isaiah 9:6-7); he is the King visited by the wise men coming from afar, who find him with his mother and adore him, offering him royal gifts (see Matthew 2:1-12).

—*her wisdom and prudence,* because our Lady is seen in the Gospel as a "wise virgin," who has chosen the better part, like Mary of Bethany (see Luke 10:42), a "teacher of truth," who hands on to the Church the saving deeds and words of her Son, which she has treasured in her heart (see Luke 2:19, 51); St. Bruno of Asti (d. 1123) writes: "Mother most wise, alone most worthy of such a Son! She kept all these words in her heart, preserving them for us and commending them to our remembrance, so that afterwards, through her teaching them, recounting them, proclaiming them, they might be recorded, preached throughout the world, and announced to all nations" (*Commentaria in Lucam,* pars I, cap. II: PL 165:355).

Entrance Antiphon

Blessed are you, holy Mary, wisest of virgins: the Word of truth was cradled in your arms; blessed are you, most prudent of virgins: you have chosen the better part.

OPENING PRAYER

A **All-holy Father, eternal God,**
in your goodness
you prepared a royal throne for your Wisdom
in the womb of the Blessed Virgin Mary;
bathe your Church
in the radiance of your life-giving Word,
that, pressing forward on its pilgrim way
in the light of your truth,
it may come to the joy
of a perfect knowledge of your love.

Grant this through our Lord Jesus Christ, your Son,
who lives and reigns with you and the Holy Spirit,
one God, for ever and ever.

B **God of wisdom,**
in your desire to restore us to your friendship
after we had lost it by sin,
you chose the Blessed Virgin Mary
as the seat of your Wisdom.

Grant through her intercession
that we may not seek the wisdom of the proud
but with humility treasure your revealed wisdom.

We ask this through our Lord Jesus Christ, your Son,
who lives and reigns with you and the Holy Spirit,
one God, for ever and ever.

PRAYER OVER THE GIFTS

**Lord,
sanctify these gifts that we offer you,
and through the intercession
of the Virgin Mary in her glory
prepare in our hearts
a worthy dwelling for your Wisdom.**

We ask this through Christ our Lord.

PREFACE

P 24 (Page 139)

Communion Antiphon

Come, eat my bread, drink the wine I have prepared for you; walk in the way of wisdom. *Proverbs 9:5, 6b*

PRAYER AFTER COMMUNION

**Lord our God,
through this holy sacrifice
pour into our hearts
the light of wisdom,
which so wonderfully filled
the heart of the Virgin Mother,
so that we may know you in truth
and love you with fidelity.**

We ask this through Christ our Lord.

25. THE BLESSED VIRGIN MARY, IMAGE AND MOTHER OF THE CHURCH

I

On 21 November 1964, at the end of the third session of the Second Vatican Council, Paul VI, during the celebration of Mass, declared our Lady "Mother of the Church, that is, of the entire Christian people, both the faithful and their pastors, who call her their most loving Mother," and decreed that "from now onward the whole Christian people should give even greater honor to the Mother of God under this most loving title" (AAS 56, 1965, p. 1015).

Accordingly, many particular Churches and religious families began to venerate the Blessed Virgin under the title of "Mother of the Church." In 1974, to encourage Marian celebrations during the Holy Year of Reconciliation (1975), this Mass was composed; it was shortly afterwards inserted in the second *editio typica* edition of *The Roman Missal (Sacramentary)* among the Votive Masses in honor of the Blessed Virgin Mary (MR, pp. 867–869).

The formulary looks at the many links between the Church and the Blessed Virgin but celebrates in particular the maternal role which God has been pleased to assign to our Lady in the Church and for the sake of the Church.

The euchological texts are especially concerned with four key events in the history of salvation:

—*the incarnation of the Word,* when Mary received the Son of God "in the purity of her heart and, conceiving (him) in her virgin womb, gave birth to our Savior and so nurtured the Church at its very beginning" (Pref);
—*the passion of Christ,* when, "hanging on the cross, (he) appointed the Blessed Virgin Mary, his mother, to be our mother also" (OP, see Pref, Com Ant, A);
—*the outpouring of the Holy Spirit* at Pentecost, when the mother of the Lord "joined her prayers with those of the apostles, . . . and so became the perfect pattern of the Church at prayer" (Pref);
—*the assumption of our Lady:* in the "glory of heaven, she cares for the pilgrim Church with a mother's love, following its progress homeward until the day of the Lord dawns in splendor" (Pref).

Entrance Antiphon

With one heart the disciples continued steadfast in prayer with Mary, the mother of Jesus, alleluia. *See Acts 1:14*

OPENING PRAYER

God of mercies,
your only Son, while hanging on the cross,
appointed the Blessed Virgin Mary, his mother,
to be our mother also.

Like her
and under her loving care,
may your Church grow day by day,
rejoice in the holiness of its children,
and so attract to itself all the peoples of the earth.

We ask this through our Lord Jesus Christ, your Son,
who lives and reigns with you and the Holy Spirit,
one God, for ever and ever.

PRAYER OVER THE GIFTS

Lord,
accept our gifts
and make them the sacrament of our salvation.

By its power
warm our hearts with the love of the Virgin Mary,
mother of the Church,
and join us more closely with her
in sharing the redeeming work of her Son.

We ask this through Christ our Lord.

PREFACE **P 25** (Page 140)

Communion Antiphon

A **As he hung upon the cross, Jesus said to the disciple whom he loved: Behold your mother.** *See John 19:26-27*

B **Blessed are you, Mary, full of grace, mother and virgin; you are a shining example of faith, hope, and love to the Church.**

PRAYER AFTER COMMUNION

Lord God,
we have received the foretaste and promise
of the fullness of redemption.

We pray that your Church,
through the intercession of the Virgin Mother,
may proclaim the Gospel to all nations
and by the power of the Spirit
reach to the ends of the earth.

We ask this through Christ our Lord.

26. THE BLESSED VIRGIN MARY, IMAGE AND MOTHER OF THE CHURCH

II

This Mass is in celebration of God the Father, who in his "infinite goodness" (Pref) has given the Church the Blessed Virgin Mary, the mother of Christ, as a "model of every virtue" (Ent Ant, Com Ant, see LG, no. 65). "Although in the Blessed Virgin the Church already attains that perfection by which she exists without spot or wrinkle (see Ephesians 5:27), the faithful are still striving to conquer sin and grow in holiness. They therefore raise their eyes to Mary, who shines brightly as the exemplar of virtues for the whole company of the elect" (LG, no. 65):

—*the model of sublime love,* so that the faithful pray: that your Church "may stand before all peoples as the sacrament of your love" (OP);
—*the model of faith and hope,* so that the faithful ask that the Church "may look always to the Blessed Virgin and so grow in fervor of faith," and be "strengthened by the hope of future glory" (PAC);
—*the model of profound humility:* ". . . you have shown us in the Blessed Virgin Mary the model of . . . profound humility" (OP);
—*the model of persevering prayer in oneness of mind and heart,* for the apostles and the first disciples "with one heart continued steadfast in prayer with Mary, the mother of Jesus" (1 Read, Acts 1:12-14); Mary "prays with the apostles in oneness of mind and heart" (Pref);
—*the model of worship in spirit:* Mary is "the shining model of true worship for your (God's) Church and of our duty to offer ourselves as a holy victim, pleasing in your (God's) eyes" (POG, see Romans 12:1);
—*the model of liturgical worship:* the mother of Jesus, as Pope Paul VI reminds us, is the "exemplar of that sense of reverent devotion with which the Church celebrates the divine mysteries and expresses them in its life" (MC, no. 16); for Mary is "the Virgin who listens, . . . the Virgin of prayer, . . . the Virgin Mother, . . . the Virgin who offers" (Pref; see MC, nos. 16–21); she is the Virgin who keeps vigil, awaiting the resurrection of her Son (see Pref). In brief, Mary is "the model of the Church as a whole in its worship of God" (MC, no. 21).

Entrance Antiphon

You are truly worthy of all praise, holy Virgin Mary; you are the mother of Christ, our God; you set before the Church a shining model of every virtue!

OPENING PRAYER

Lord God,
you have shown us in the Blessed Virgin Mary
the model of sublime love and profound humility;
grant that your Church may be like her,
obedient to your commandment of love,
so that by giving itself wholeheartedly
to seeking your glory and to serving others
it may stand before all peoples
as the sacrament of your love.

We ask this through our Lord Jesus Christ, your Son,
who lives and reigns with you and the Holy Spirit,
one God, for ever and ever.

PRAYER OVER THE GIFTS

Lord,
transform these gifts,
which we bring to you with joyful hearts,
into the sacrament of our salvation
on this memorial of the Virgin Mary in glory;
for she is the shining model
of true worship for your Church
and of our duty to offer ourselves
as a holy victim, pleasing in your eyes.

We ask this through Christ our Lord.

PREFACE **P 26** (Page 141)

Communion Antiphon

Blessed are you, Mary, full of grace: we lift up our eyes to you as a shining model of every virtue to the whole company of those whom God has chosen!

PRAYER AFTER COMMUNION

Lord God,
we have offered to you in sacrifice
the holy mysteries of your table
and have received with loving hearts
the body and blood of your Son;
grant that your Church
may look always to the Blessed Virgin
and so grow in fervor of faith,
be confirmed in love,
and be strengthened by the hope of future glory.

We ask this through Christ our Lord.

27. THE BLESSED VIRGIN MARY, IMAGE AND MOTHER OF THE CHURCH

III

This Mass celebrates God's goodness in loving the Church so much that the Blessed Virgin is set before its eyes as the prophetic image of its pilgrimage on earth and of its future glory in heaven. In the words of the Second Vatican Council, "in her the Church holds up and admires the most excellent effect of the redemption and joyfully contemplates, as in a flawless image, that which the Church itself desires and hopes wholly to be" (SC, art. 103).

The Blessed Virgin, as "the spotless mirror of God's glory" (Com Ant, A, see Wisdom 7:26; see Ent Ant), provides the Church with a most faithful image of the perfect disciple, the pure virgin, the faithful bride, the loving mother, the queen crowned with glory. The liturgy therefore celebrates the Blessed Virgin as:

—*the disciple* who is perfect in the following of Christ. We pray then that the Church, "with eyes fixed on Mary, . . . may follow closely in the footsteps of her Son" (OP), and be fashioned more and more "in that image of Christ, which it admires and praises in his glorious mother" (POG);

—"*a virgin* unsurpassed in purity of faith" (Pref), whom the Church always strives to imitate: for "she is herself a virgin who keeps whole and unsullied the faith she has given to her Bridegroom" (LG, no. 64);

—"*a bride* joined to Christ in an unbreakable bond of love and united with him in his suffering" (Pref); as the Church, "contemplates her in the light of the Word truly made flesh" it reverently enters more deeply into the surpassing mystery of the incarnation and takes on more and more the image of its Bridegroom" (LG, no. 65);

—"*a mother* by the overshadowing of the Holy Spirit, filled with loving concern for all her children" (Pref); the Church, by "imitating her love and faithfully carrying out the will of the Father and through the word of God it has faithfully received, itself becomes a mother. For by preaching and baptism it brings forth to new and immortal life children conceived by the Holy Spirit and born of God" (LG, no. 64);

—"*a queen* adorned with the jewels of grace, . . . sharing eternally in the glory of her Lord" (Pref); "as the Church looks on (Mary) it sees the perfect image of its future glory" (Ent Ant, see SC, art. 103; see POG, Pref).

Entrance Antiphon

Hail, holy Mary, mirror without stain! As the Church looks on you it sees the perfect image of its future glory.

OPENING PRAYER

**Lord our God,
through your power and goodness
the Blessed Virgin,
the fairest fruit of your redeeming love,
shines forth as the perfect image of the Church;
grant to your people on their pilgrim way on earth
that, with eyes fixed on Mary,
they may follow closely in the footsteps of her Son
until they come to that fullness of glory,
which now they contemplate in his mother
with hearts filled with joy.**

**We ask this through our Lord Jesus Christ, your Son,
who lives and reigns with you and the Holy Spirit,
one God, for ever and ever.**

PRAYER OVER THE GIFTS

**Lord,
grant that this offering, consecrated to your glory,
may purify your people
and fashion your Church more and more
in that image of Christ,
which it admires and praises in his glorious mother.**

We ask this through Christ our Lord.

PREFACE **P 27** (Page 143)

Communion Antiphon

A **Virgin Mary, you are the brightness of eternal light, the spotless mirror of God's glory, the image of his goodness.** *See Wisdom 7:26*

B **You shall conceive and bear a son; you shall call his name Jesus.** *Luke 1:31*

PRAYER AFTER COMMUNION

Lord God,
grant that your Church,
strengthened through the power of this sacrament,
may eagerly follow the way of the Gospel
until it comes to that joyful vision of peace
which the Virgin Mary, your lowly handmaid,
already enjoys in her unending glory.

We ask this through Christ our Lord.

28. THE IMMACULATE HEART OF THE BLESSED VIRGIN MARY

The Roman liturgy celebrates the memorial of the Immaculate Heart of the Blessed Virgin Mary with a special formulary on the Saturday after the second Sunday after Pentecost. Several Masses, however, are to be found in honor of the Immaculate Heart of Mary in the propers of Masses of particular Churches and religious institutes, celebrating different aspects of this devotion. The formulary set out here is largely drawn from the *Proprium Congregationis Missionariorum Filiorum Immaculati Cordis beatae Virginis* (see *Annales Congregationis* 52, 1976, pp. 363–365).

The meaning of "the heart of the Virgin" is to be understood in a biblical sense: it denotes the person of the Blessed Virgin herself; her intimate and unique being; the center and source of her interior life, of her mind and memory, of her will and love; the single-mindedness with which she loved God and the disciples and devoted herself wholeheartedly to the saving work of her Son.

The formulary celebrates the loving kindness of God, who, after giving to the Church the heart of our Lord Jesus Christ as a proof of his love, gave it also the heart of the Blessed Virgin Mary to be contemplated as the model of the "new heart" of one who lives by the "New Covenant."

The heart of the Blessed Virgin, who, filled with faith and love, received the Word of God, is called in the first place the "home of (God's) eternal Word" (OP), and the "sanctuary of the Holy Spirit" (OP, see LG, no. 53), because of the divine Spirit dwelling always within her. It is described as "*immaculate*" (OP), that is, free from the stain of sin; as "*wise*" (Pref), because the Blessed Virgin, linking prophecy to fact, treasured in her heart the memory of the words and deeds belonging to the mystery of salvation (see Luke 2:19, 51); as "*obedient*" (Pref, see 1 Kings 3:9), because her heart willingly united itself to the will of God (see Luke 1:48); as "*new*" (Pref), in accordance with the prophecy of Ezekiel (see Ezekiel 18:31; 36:26), clothed in the newness of grace through the anticipated merits of Christ (see Ephesians 4:23-24); as "*gentle*" (Pref), like the heart of Christ as he invites us: "Learn from me, for I am gentle and humble of heart" (Matthew 11:29); as "*undivided*" (Pref), that is, free from all duplicity and imbued with the Spirit of truth; as "*pure*" or, as in the Beatitudes (see Matthew 5:8), capable of seeing God; as "*steadfast*" (Pref) in embracing the will of God, when, as Simeon prophesied (see Luke 2:35), persecution threatened her Son (see Matthew 2:13) or his death was imminent (see John 19:25); as "*watchful*" (Pref), for, like the heart of the beloved in the Song of Songs (see 5:2), when Christ lay asleep in the sepulcher, her heart kept vigil, waiting for his resurrection.

Entrance Antiphon

In me is all the grace of the way and the truth, in me is all hope of life and of strength. *Sirach 24:25*

OPENING PRAYER

Lord our God,
you made the immaculate heart of the Blessed Virgin Mary
the home of your eternal Word
and the sanctuary of the Holy Spirit.
Give us a heart
that is free from sin
and attentive to your will,
that, faithful to your commandments,
we may love you above all things
and seek to help others in their need.

We ask this through our Lord Jesus Christ, your Son,
who lives and reigns with you and the Holy Spirit,
one God, for ever and ever.

PRAYER OVER THE GIFTS

Lord,
look with favor on the gifts we bring
as we celebrate this memorial
of the Blessed Virgin Mary;
grant that, as we follow her example,
we may faithfully cherish and continually ponder
the riches of grace that we owe to your Son,
who lives and reigns for ever and ever.

PREFACE **P 28** (Page 144)

Communion Antiphon

Mary treasured all these words and pondered them in her heart.

Luke 2:19

PRAYER AFTER COMMUNION

**Lord our God,
you have given us a share in eternal redemption;
grant that we who celebrate
the memory of the mother of your Son
may rejoice in the fullness of your grace
and experience a continuous increase
of your saving power.**

We ask this through Christ our Lord.

29. THE BLESSED VIRGIN MARY, QUEEN OF ALL CREATION

In 1954 the feast of the Queenship of Mary was instituted by Pius XII, to be celebrated on 31 May. In 1969 Paul VI, promulgating the new General Roman Calendar, appropriately transferred the feast to 22 August, the octave of the Assumption. The royal dignity of our Lady is part of the mystery of her full glorification and perfect conformity with her Son, the King of all the ages. In the words of the Second Vatican Council, "the Immaculate Virgin, . . . when she had completed her earthly life, was taken up body and soul into the glory of heaven and exalted as the queen of all creation, so that she might be more fully conformed to her Son, the Lord of lords (see Revelation 19:16) and victor over sin and death" (LG, no. 59).

As the kingdom of Christ "is not of this world" (John 18:36), so too the royal dignity of our Lady does not belong to the order of nature, but to that of grace. Among the qualities that make up her royal dignity in the order of grace the texts of the Mass celebrate four in particular: her humility, her role as mother, her earnest intercession, her function as a sign of the future glory of the Church.

Our Lady is *the queen gloriously reigning* in heaven, because she was on earth the lowly handmaid (see Luke 1:38, 48): in the words of our Lord, "those who humble themselves will be exalted" (Luke 14:11). As God the Father has crowned Christ with glory and honor (see Pref; Psalm 8:6), after he humbled himself even to accepting death (see Pref; Philippians 2:8), and as he has seated him at his right hand (see Pref; Psalm 8:6), so he has exalted his lowly handmaid above all the choirs of angels (see Pref).

She is *queen and mother,* because she became the mother of the messianic King, who sits "on the throne of David and rules over his kingdom" (Isaiah 9:6; see 1 Read, Isaiah 9:1- 3, 5-6; Gos, Luke 1:26-38); and, by the will of God, she is our mother also, as the Church testifies: "Father, you have given us the mother of your Son to be our queen and mother" (OP).

She is *the queen who intercedes,* exalted "above all the choirs of angels," reigning in glory with her Son, interceding for all God's children, our advocate of grace, and the queen of all creation (see Pref; see LG, no. 62).

She is *the queen who is the sign of the Church in its future glory,* because what has been accomplished in her as a member surpassing all others will be accomplished in all the members of Christ's Mystical Body. It is right, therefore, for the Church to ask the intercession of our Lady that its members may share "the glory of (God's) children in the kingdom of heaven" (OP).

The formulary of this Mass is taken from *The Roman Missal (Sacramentary),* 22 August; the preface echoes the prayer for the crowning of an image of our Lady (see *Order of Crowning an Image of the Blessed Virgin Mary,* English ed., pp. 15–16).

Entrance Antiphon

The queen stands at your right hand arrayed in cloth of gold.

Psalm 45:10

OPENING PRAYER

Father,
you have given us the mother of your Son
to be our queen and mother.
With the support of her prayers
may we come to share the glory of your children
in the kingdom of heaven.

We ask this through our Lord Jesus Christ, your Son,
who lives and reigns with you and the Holy Spirit,
one God, for ever and ever.

PRAYER OVER THE GIFTS

Lord,
celebrating this memorial of the Virgin Mary,
we offer you our gifts and prayers;
may Christ, who offered himself as a perfect sacrifice,
bring all people the peace and love of your kingdom,
where he lives and reigns for ever and ever.

PREFACE **P 29** (Page 145)

Communion Antiphon

Blessed are you for firmly believing that the promises of the Lord would be fulfilled. *Luke 1:45*

PRAYER AFTER COMMUNION

We have received this heavenly sacrament
and now pray, Lord our God,
that we who honor the memory of the Blessed Virgin Mary
may come to share in the eternal banquet.

We ask this through Christ our Lord.

Section 2

This section contains nine Mass formularies for the celebration of a memorial of the Mother of the Lord under titles that refer to her cooperation in fostering the spiritual life of the faithful.

30. THE BLESSED VIRGIN MARY, MOTHER AND MEDIATRIX OF GRACE

In 1921 Pope Benedict XV (d. 1922), at the request of Cardinal Désiré Joseph Mercier (d. 1926), granted the whole of Belgium an Office and Mass of the Blessed Virgin Mary, Mediatrix of All Graces, to be celebrated on 31 May. This Office and Mass were extended by the Holy See to many other dioceses and religious institutes at their own request, so that the commemoration of our Lady as mediatrix became almost universal.

The Second Vatican Council in 1964 treated at some length the role of our Lady in the mystery of Christ and of the Church and gave a careful explanation of the meaning and force of her "mediation": "The maternal role of Mary in relation to the human family in no way obscures or lessens the unique mediation of Christ but rather demonstrates its power. Any saving influence of the Blessed Virgin on men and women is due not to any intrinsic necessity but to God's good pleasure. It flows from the superabundance of Christ's merits, is founded on his mediation, is entirely dependent on it, and from it derives its whole efficacy. It does not in any way impede but rather fosters the immediate union of the faithful with Christ" (LG, no. 60).

In 1971 the Congregation for Divine Worship approved a Mass of the Blessed Virgin Mary, Mother and Mediatrix of Grace. This Mass, faithfully following the teaching of the Second Vatican Council, commemorates both the maternal role of our Lady and her function of mediation (see *Proprium missarum Ordinis Fratrum Servorum beatae Mariae Virginis,* Curia Generalis OSM, Rome, 1972, pp. 36–37). Currently this Mass is celebrated in many places on 8 May, and, with some changes and the addition of a preface, is set out here.

The formulary rightly gives pride of place to Christ, "truly God and truly human . . . the one mediator . . . always living to make intercession for us" (Pref; see 1 Timothy 2:5; Hebrews 7:25; POG, PAC). It also commemorates our Lady as "mother of the author of all grace," for God the Father, in his "eternal wisdom and love" (OP; see Pref), chose her as the mother and companion of the Redeemer (see OP, Pref).

—The Virgin Mary is *mother of grace,* for in her "chaste womb" she carried him who is "truly God and truly human" (Ent Ant, A), and brought forth for us "the author of all grace" (OP; see *All*).

—The Virgin Mary is *mediatrix of grace,* for she was the handmaid of Christ in gaining for us the greatest of all graces: redemption and salvation, the divine life and unending glory (see LG, no. 61).

In the formulary the "mediation" of our Lady is correctly interpreted as "the love that she bestows as a mother" (Pref): "of intercession and pardon, of prayer and grace, of reconciliation and peace" (Pref).

Entrance Antiphon

A **Hail, holy Mary, rich fountain of love, treasure-house of all graces, in your chaste womb you bore him who is truly God and truly human.**

B **Hail, holy Mother of God, our life was lost but now through you it is restored, for you received a child from heaven and brought to birth the Savior of the world.**

OPENING PRAYER

Lord our God,
in your eternal wisdom and love
you chose the Blessed Virgin Mary
to be the mother of the author of all grace
and as his companion in bringing about
the mystery of our redemption.
Grant that she may obtain for us
graces in abundance
and lead us at last
to the harbor of eternal salvation.

We ask this through our Lord Jesus Christ, your Son,
who lives and reigns with you and the Holy Spirit,
one God, for ever and ever.

PRAYER OVER THE GIFTS

Lord,
receive our offering of peace and praise
on this memorial of the Virgin Mary in glory;
by the power of the Holy Spirit
make what we present the sacrament of our redemption,
so that what Christ our mediator has established
as the means of our reconciliation with you
may become for us the source of grace
and the enduring fountain of eternal salvation.

We ask this through Christ our Lord.

PREFACE **P 30** (Page 146)

Communion Antiphon

The Spirit and the Bride say: Come. Let all who hear say: Come. Let all who thirst, come; let all who will, take the free gift of the water of life. *Revelation 22:17*

PRAYER AFTER COMMUNION

**Refreshed, Lord God,
at the fountain of salvation,
we pray that by the power of this sacrament
and through the prayers of the Blessed Virgin
we may be more closely united
to Christ, the mediator,
and ever more faithfully enter into
the mystery of redemption.**

We ask this through Christ our Lord.

31. THE BLESSED VIRGIN MARY, FOUNTAIN OF SALVATION

The Mother of the Lord is frequently honored under the title of "fountain" in the liturgies of East and West. She is called "fountain of living water," "fountain of charity," "fountain of clemency," "fountain of grace," "fountain of mercy," "fountain enclosed" (see 1 Read, Song of Songs 4:12), "fountain of salvation" (see G. G. Meersseman, *Der Hymnos Akathistos im Abendland,* Vol. 2, Universitätsverlag, Freiburg, Switzerland, 1960, pp. 309–310).

There are a number of sanctuaries dedicated to our Lady under the title of "fountain," often with a spring of water used by the faithful on pilgrimage. The most celebrated of these in the East is the sanctuary of the Mother of God of the Living Fountain in Constantinople, erected in the sixth century. In the West there is the sanctuary at Lourdes, beside the cave where our Lady appeared to St. Bernadette Soubirous and caused a spring of water to gush forth.

This formulary celebrates:

—*the divine motherhood of our Lady,* for it was through her that God opened for us "the fountain of salvation" (OP): "in the great mystery of the incarnation . . . she brought forth (God's) eternal Word, Jesus Christ, the fountain of living water" (Pref). He is the true temple of God (see John 2:21), from which the saving waters come forth, healing all whom they touch (see 1 Read, Ezekiel 47:1-2, 8-9, 12); he invites the thirsty to come to him and drink (see Com Ant, A, John 7:37), that is, those who believe in him are to receive the gift of the Holy Spirit (see John 7:39); he is the rock (see 1 Corinthians 10:4), struck by the lance, from which "immediately came out blood and water" (Gos, John 19:25-37);

—*the spiritual maternity of the Church:* for the Church, as a wise mother, satisfies the thirst of the faithful by giving them "the waters flowing from Christ's side. These are the rich, life-giving waters served in the sacraments" (Pref), especially in the eucharistic banquet, at which the faithful draw "water in joy from the fountain of the Savior" (PAC, see Resp, Isaiah 12:3), and "the sacrament we (they) have received" becomes "a spring of water welling up to eternal life" (PAC);

—*the outpouring of the Holy Spirit,* which is frequently symbolized in Scripture as the outpouring of water. The entrance antiphon (A) recalls the words of Isaiah: "I will pour water over the thirsty land, I will pour my Spirit on your descendants, my blessing on your children" (see Isaiah 44:3). The fountain from which the water flows is Christ himself (as in the opening prayer, "grant that we who celebrate the memory of our Lady may always draw from this wellspring of life and bring forth a rich harvest of the fruits of the Holy Spirit") and the sacraments instituted by (Christ), by which the faithful as they receive them are "filled with the Holy Spirit" (Pref).

Several texts of this formulary, and the alternative readings for the liturgy of the word, are taken from the *Proprio de la misa y de la liturgia de las horas de la diócesis de Cartagena,* Cartagena, 1985, pp. 32–34.

Entrance Antiphon

A **I will pour water over the thirsty land, I will pour my Spirit on your descendants, my blessing on your children, and they will grow like poplars beside flowing streams.** *See Isaiah 44:3-4*

B **The streams of a river make glad the city of God, the holy dwelling-place of the Most High. God is within the city; it will remain unshaken for ever.** *Psalm 46:5-6a*

OPENING PRAYER

**All-holy Lord and Father,
through the Blessed Virgin Mary
you have unsealed for us the fountain of salvation,
Jesus Christ, your Son;
grant that we who celebrate the memory of our Lady
may always draw from this wellspring of life
and bring forth a rich harvest
of the fruits of the Holy Spirit.**

**We ask this through our Lord Jesus Christ, your Son,
who lives and reigns with you and the Holy Spirit,
one God, for ever and ever.**

PRAYER OVER THE GIFTS

**Lord,
change into the sacrament of salvation
the gifts we joyously present
on this memorial of the most holy Virgin Mary,
for it was through her intercession
that your Son worked the first of his great signs,
changing an abundance of water into wine.**

We ask this through Christ our Lord.

PREFACE **P 31** (Page 147)

Communion Antiphon

A **Let anyone who thirsts and believes in me, says the Lord, come to me and drink.** *John 7:37*

B **All you that thirst, come to the waters; buy and eat, come, buy wine and milk, without payment, without cost.** *Isaiah 55:1*

PRAYER AFTER COMMUNION

Lord God,
you have refreshed us
at your banquet of salvation
where we have drawn water in joy
from the fountain of the Savior;
grant that as we celebrate the memory of blessed Mary
the sacrament we have received
may be a spring of water welling up to eternal life.

We ask this through Christ our Lord.

32. THE BLESSED VIRGIN MARY, MOTHER AND TEACHER IN THE SPIRIT

The Carmelite brothers and sisters, both those of the ancient observance and those of the reform of St. Teresa of Jesus (d. 1582), have at all times been zealous in spreading far and wide the love of prayer, the desire for evangelical perfection, and devotion to the Mother of Christ.

Their special devotion is to the Blessed Virgin under the title of "Our Lady of Mount Carmel": as they make their journey to the "holy mountain, which is Christ" (OP), she cherishes them as a loving mother, protects them as a sure patroness, and accompanies them as a faithful sister. The Carmelites, though they are assiduous in meditating on the totality of the mystery of the Blessed Virgin Mary, are particularly devoted to contemplation of our Lady intent on prayer, or leading her hidden life, or treasuring the words of the Lord in her heart, or doing her works of charity.

Our Lady has always been known by the Carmelite brothers and sisters as "mother and teacher in the Spirit" because she was a perfect disciple of Christ and "is still a mother, continuing to give (God) children . . . , encouraging them by her love, and drawing them by her example to pursue perfect charity" (Pref).

In this formulary our Lady is celebrated as:

—*a teacher,* who keeps the words of the Lord in her heart (see *All,* Com Ant, Luke 2:19, 51), who "instructs by her example" (POG), teaching "fear of the Lord" (Ent Ant, see Psalm 34:12); who, since she is "the model of all who live by the spirit of the Gospel" (Pref), teaches us, "as we look up to her in prayer . . . to love (God) above all things," to be "rapt in contemplation" of his Word, and untiringly to "serve the needs of others" (Pref);

—*a mother,* who gently invites us to "go up to the mountain of the Lord" (Ent Ant; see Isaiah 2:3), which is Christ himself (see OP); a mother through whom Wisdom says: "Those who find me, will find life" (Proverbs 8:34; see 1 Read, Proverbs 8:17-21, 34-35); a mother, who accepted us as her children at the foot of the cross (see Gos, John 19:25-27), who "watches over (us) by her patronage" (POG) and keeps us "under her protection" (OP).

With some changes, this Mass is taken from the *Proprium missarum Fratrum Discalceatorum Ordinis b.mae Mariae Virginis de Monte Carmelo,* Curia Generalis OCD, Rome, 1973, pp. 51–52, 90.

Entrance Antiphon

Come, to me, children, and listen: I will teach you the fear of the Lord. Come, let us go up to the mountain of the Lord, and we shall walk in his ways. *Psalm 34:12; Isaiah 2:3*

OPENING PRAYER

**Lord,
let the blessed intercession of the glorious Virgin Mary
come to our aid,
so that, under her protection,
we may reach the holy mountain,
which is Christ,
who lives and reigns with you and the Holy Spirit,
one God, for ever and ever.**

PRAYER OVER THE GIFTS

**Lord,
we offer these gifts from joyful hearts;
through them sanctify your servants,
whom the Blessed Virgin instructs by her example
and watches over by her patronage,
so that, faithful to our baptismal promises,
we may serve you and our neighbor with sincerity of heart.**

We ask this through Christ our Lord.

PREFACE **P 32** (Page 148)

Communion Antiphon

Mary treasured all these words and pondered them in her heart.
Luke 2:19

PRAYER AFTER COMMUNION

Lord God,
you have given us new strength
through the sacrament
of the sacred body and precious blood of your Son;
grant that this gift of your love
may be our lasting protection
and inspire us to follow faithfully
in the footsteps of the Blessed Virgin Mary
by imitating her virtues.

We ask this through Christ our Lord.

33. THE BLESSED VIRGIN MARY, MOTHER OF GOOD COUNSEL

Whenever the faithful throughout the world recite the Litany of Loreto, they invoke the Blessed Virgin as mother of good counsel, a title Leo XIII inserted into the Litany in 1903. Largely through the work of the brothers and sisters of the Augustinian family, devotion to the mother of good counsel has spread far and wide from the town of Genazzano, not far from Rome, which has a famous sanctuary dedicated to her.

Our Lady is rightly honored under this title, for she is the mother of Christ, whom Isaiah with prophetic vision called "Wonderful Counselor" (Isaiah 9:5, see 1 Read, Isaiah 9:1-3, 5-6; PAC); she lived her whole life under the guidance of the "Spirit of counsel," who "overshadowed" her (POG); she "gave herself wholeheartedly to (God's) wise and loving plan for renewing all things in Christ" (Pref; see Ephesians 1:10); "generously (God) poured out" on her "the gifts of (the) Holy Spirit" (Pref), principal among which is the "spirit of wisdom" (Ent Ant; see Wisdom 7:7b).

In the texts of this Mass our Lady, enlightened by the gift of counsel, is honored as mother and teacher as she cries out in gratitude in the words of Wisdom itself: "To me belong counsel and prudence, understanding and strength are mine" (*All,* Proverbs 8:14); gifts willingly shared with the children and disciples of Wisdom (see Ent Ant), whom Mary instructs that they must before all else do what Christ has told them to do (see Gos, John 2:1-11; Com Ant, John 2:5).

In celebrating this Mass we earnestly ask God for the gift of counsel, to teach us how to know his will and to guide us in all we do (OP; see PAC).

This Mass, except for the preface, is taken from the *Proprium missarum Ordinis Fratrum sancti Augustini,* approved in 1975 by the Congregation for Divine Worship.

Entrance Antiphon

I called upon God, and there came to me the spirit of wisdom; I learned wisdom in simplicity of heart, I hand it on ungrudgingly, I do not hide away its riches. *Wisdom 7:7b, 13*

OPENING PRAYER

Lord,
you know that our thoughts on earth
are full of fear and uncertainty;
through the intercession of the Blessed Virgin Mary,
from whom your Son took flesh and blood,
send us the gift of counsel
to teach us how to discern your will
and to guide us in all we do.

Grant this through our Lord Jesus Christ, your Son,
who lives and reigns with you and the Holy Spirit,
one God, for ever and ever.

PRAYER OVER THE GIFTS

Lord,
let the Spirit of counsel,
who so wonderfully overshadowed your handmaid,
the Blessed Virgin,
come upon the gifts we present in worship
and make them pleasing to you.

We ask this through Christ our Lord.

PREFACE **P 33** (Page 149)

Communion Antiphon

The mother of Jesus said to the attendants: Do whatever he tells you.

See John 2:5

PRAYER AFTER COMMUNION

**Lord our God,
we have shared in your mysteries
on this memorial of our Lady, mother of good counsel.**

**Grant that we may learn what is pleasing to you
and receive salvation from your Son,
whom you gave us through the Blessed Virgin Mary
to be our Wonderful Counselor.**

We ask this through Christ our Lord.

34. THE BLESSED VIRGIN MARY, CAUSE OF OUR JOY

Christ Jesus came into the world to bring peace and joy to the human family (see John 15:11; 17:13). At his birth he filled the humble shepherds with joy (see Luke 2:10), at his resurrection he brought joy to the disciples (see John 20:20; Luke 24:41), at his ascension he left the apostles in great joy (see Luke 24:52); from his place at the right hand of the Father he sent upon the infant Church the Spirit of love and joy (see Galatians 5:22).

The Church as the Bride of Christ has always found joy in its Bridegroom and returned his love with ever-increasing joy. Since Jesus had come to us through Mary, the Church came gradually to understand that the Blessed Virgin, because of her cooperation in the incarnation of the Word, is the cause or origin or source of this great joy; the Church has known too that the sorrow brought into the world by Eve's disobedience has been changed into joy by Mary's obedience, and so it began to honor her with the title "cause of our joy." Devotion to our Lady under this title has developed especially in France and Canada *(Notre Dame de Liesse)*.

The texts of this Mass recall the saving actions of God through Christ in the Holy Spirit that have brought joy to the Blessed Virgin or to the Church or to humanity. The texts celebrate in particular:

—*the choice of our Lady,* who from eternity "found favor with God" (Ent Ant, see Luke 1:30), and was chosen as God's dwelling place ("See, I come and will dwell in the midst of you" [1 Read, A, Zechariah 2:14]), as "the city of God" made glad by "the streams of a river" (Com Ant, Psalm 46:5); and therefore as the city-bride clothed "in the garments of salvation" and robed "in the vesture of justice" (see 1 Read, B, Isaiah 61:10). Hence in the Mass resound joyful voices: "Rejoice, Virgin Mary" (Ent Ant, see Luke 1:28); "Rejoice and be glad, daughter of Zion" (1 Read, A, Zechariah 2:14); "Hail, . . . joy of humankind" *(All)*;

—*the birth of the Virgin,* which "heralded joy for all the world" (Pref);

—*the visit of Mary to Elizabeth,* when our Lady spoke her canticle of joy and jubilation (see Resp, Luke 1:46-48, 49-50, 53-54) and the infant John leapt in his mother's womb because of the coming of the Savior (see Gos, Luke 1:39-47);

—*the birth of our Lord,* for God was pleased to bring "joy to the world through the incarnation of (his) Son" (OP); the motherhood of the Virgin "brought forth (to us) the true Light" (Pref), and also "salvation and joy" *(All)*;

—*the resurrection of Christ:* for we pray to God that we may be guided to eternal happiness "through the saving power of (Christ's) resurrection" (PAC);

—*the assumption of our Lady:* for "her passing into glory raised her to the heights of heaven, where . . . she waits for us with loving care until we too enjoy the vision of (God's) glory for ever" (Pref).

Entrance Antiphon

Rejoice, Virgin Mary, you have found favor with God! Listen; you will conceive and bear a son and you shall call his name Jesus.

See Luke 1:28, 30-31

OPENING PRAYER

Lord our God,
you were pleased to bring joy to the world
through the incarnation of your Son.

Grant that we who honor his mother,
the cause of our joy,
may always walk in the way of your commandments
with our hearts set on true and lasting joy.

We ask this through our Lord Jesus Christ, your Son,
who lives and reigns with you and the Holy Spirit,
one God, for ever and ever.

PRAYER OVER THE GIFTS

Lord,
receive the offerings of your joyful Church,
and as you have given us every good gift
in Christ the Savior,
born of the immaculate Virgin,
grant us a share in his harvest of everlasting joy.

We ask this through Christ our Lord.

PREFACE **P 34** (Page 150)

Communion Antiphon

A **The streams of a river make glad the city of God, the holy dwelling-place of the Most High.** *Psalm 46:5*

B **All generations will call me blessed: the Almighty has done great things for me, and holy is his Name.**

PRAYER AFTER COMMUNION

Lord God,
we profess as truly God and truly human
the child conceived by the Virgin Mary.
Seal in our hearts the mysteries of true faith
and through the saving power of the resurrection
guide us to eternal happiness.

We ask this through Christ our Lord.

35. THE BLESSED VIRGIN MARY, PILLAR OF FAITH

The Blessed Virgin is a woman of outstanding faith, a disciple who in a certain sense sums up and reechoes in her own person the main themes of Christian teaching (see LG, no. 65), a mother supporting and protecting the faith of her children.

—*A woman of outstanding faith:* Elizabeth, the mother of the Precursor, called her blessed for her belief in God's message (see Luke 1:45); she conceived God's Son in faith and, supported by faith, she followed Jesus and stood beside the cross, enduring the sight of his death; in faith she believed that he would rise again, and waited for the coming of the Spirit, promised by the Father.

—*A disciple summing up in her own person the teachings of the faith:* our Lady, as the Second Vatican Council proclaims, "was intimately involved in the history of salvation, and in a certain sense unites and reflects in her own person the chief teachings of the faith" (LG, no. 65); her immaculate conception shows the freedom and munificence of God in choosing the instruments of salvation and grace; her consent to the work of salvation in the incarnation proclaims the meaning and power of human cooperation in God's saving plan; the virginal birth of Christ shows that he is truly God and truly human; her holiness and her state of life—as virgin, wife, and mother—sketch out the features of the Church; her assumption prefigures the future glory of the human race.

—*A mother supporting the faith of her children:* our Lady, gloriously reigning in heaven, works in a mysterious way on earth, as she points out to her children the way of truth. It has often happened that where love and devotion toward Mary were strong the people have kept the faith even though they were deprived of all spiritual help.

The glorious Mother of God, who destroys all heresies, who undoes the power of error and exposes the falsehood of idols (see the Hymn *Akathistos,* vv. 111–112; ed. G. G. Meersseman, *Der Hymnos Akathistos im Abendland,* vol. 1, Universitätsverlag, Freiburg, Switzerland, 1958, p. 114), has in consequence been invoked by the Christian people from very early times as a "pillar of faith."

This Mass, in which we ask that we may be "steadfast in faith" (POG) and "strong in faith" (OP) and "true to the faith on earth" (PAC), reproduces in great part the Mass of "Nuestra Señora del Pilar" (see *Misal Romano reformado por mandato del Concilio Vaticano II . . . , editio typica* approved by the episcopal conference of Spain, Coeditores Liturgicos, Madrid, 1978, pp. 659–660).

Entrance Antiphon

A **Mary, Virgin Mother, you are like the pillar of light that, day and night, went before God's people to direct their footsteps through the wilderness.** *See Wisdom 18:3; Exodus 13:21-22*

B **Mother of Christ, queen in glory, you conceived your Son in faith and believed that after dying for us he would rise again; you show yourself a loving mother to the Church and a pillar of its faith.**

OPENING PRAYER

Almighty and eternal God,
you gave the Blessed Virgin Mary,
glorious mother of your Son,
as a pillar of strength
to all who call upon her aid;
grant through her intercession
that we may be strong in faith,
unwavering in hope,
and steadfast in love.

We ask this through our Lord Jesus Christ, your Son,
who lives and reigns with you and the Holy Spirit,
one God, for ever and ever.

PRAYER OVER THE GIFTS

Lord, all-holy Father,
you have enlightened our minds
with the light of faith;
grant that,
through the intercession of the loving mother
of the Redeemer,
our offerings and prayers
may keep us steadfast in faith
and untiring in love.

We ask this through Christ our Lord.

PREFACE **P 35** (Page 151)

Communion Antiphon

From this day all generations will call me blessed: the Almighty has done great things for me. *Luke 1:48*

PRAYER AFTER COMMUNION

Lord our God,
present in your Church in many ways,
we thank you for the sacrament we have received
and pray that, with the support of the Blessed Virgin Mary,
we may be true to the faith on earth
and so enjoy the vision of your glory in heaven.

We ask this through Christ our Lord.

36. THE BLESSED VIRGIN MARY, MOTHER OF FAIREST LOVE

In the *Missale Romanum* (1962), which remained in force until the promulgation of the Missal revised in accordance with the norms of the Second Vatican Council (1970), there is a Mass of Blessed Mary, Queen of Saints and Mother of Fairest Love, in the section, *Pro aliquibis locis* (for certain places), celebrated on 8 May (earlier on 31 May).

The expression ''mother of fairest love'' is found in the Vulgate text of Sirach 24:24 (''I am the mother of fairest love, of reverence, of knowledge, and of holy hope''): from the tenth century it has been frequently used in Masses of our Lady.

In this Mass the Church, following tradition of both East and West, as it celebrates the mystery and role of our Lady, contemplates with joy her spiritual beauty. Beauty is the radiance of the holiness and truth of God, ''the origin of all beauty'' (see OP, B), and it is the image of the goodness and fidelity of Christ, ''fairest of all (God's) children on earth'' (OP, A; Psalm 45:3).

In this formulary the Blessed Virgin is called ''beautiful'' for three reasons: because as ''full of grace'' (Gos, Luke 1:28) and ''adorned with the gifts of the Holy Spirit'' (OP, C), she ''is resplendent . . . with the glory of her Son and the beauty of holiness'' (OP, B); because she loved God, her Son, in all his radiance, and all members of the human race, with a love that was full of beauty, that is, with a love that was virginal, bridal, and maternal; because she shared so beautifully in the mystery of the conception and birth of Christ and his death and resurrection (see Pref), that is, she shared in God's saving plan with courage and gentleness, with cooperation and fidelity.

To celebrate our Lady's spiritual beauty, the formulary makes use of biblical and patristic figures and images customary in the liturgy. In our Lady, who is ''all fair'' and in whom there is ''no blemish'' (see Resp, Song of Songs 4:7), are found in the highest degree the celebrated virtues of the women of the Old Testament: the beauty and love of the bride in the Song of Songs (see Ent Ant, B, Song of Songs 6:10; Resp); the beauty and wisdom of Judith (see Com Ant, A, Judith 11:21); the splendor and grace of the Queen, the Bride of the messianic King (see Com Ant, Psalm 45:3).

The ''way of beauty'' is the way of Christian perfection: the faithful, as they walk ''with the Blessed Virgin'' (see POG), strive to ''walk always in the ways of (God's) justice'' (PAC) and ask God that they may ''turn away from the ugliness of sin and love only the beauty that comes from (the) Spirit'' (OP, C).

Entrance Antiphon

A **Go forth, daughters of Zion, and see your queen; the morning stars sing her praises, sun and moon bow before her beauty, and all God's children rejoice in her presence.**

B **Daughter of Zion, full of loveliness and grace, you are fair as the moon, glorious as the sun, most favored of all women.**

See Song of Songs 6:10; Luke 1:42

OPENING PRAYER

A **Lord our God,**
by the wonder of your wisdom
Jesus Christ, the Bridegroom of the Church
and fairest of all your children on earth,
came forth from a virgin's womb;
through the intercession of his mother in her glory
give joy and peace to all peoples
and fill our hearts with the light of your holiness.

We ask this through our Lord Jesus Christ, your Son,
who lives and reigns with you and the Holy Spirit,
one God, for ever and ever.

B **Lord God,**
your lowly handmaid, the Virgin Mary,
is resplendent in your presence
with the glory of her Son and the beauty of holiness;
grant that like her
we may seek only what is true and just
and so come before you, the origin of all beauty
and the author of purest love.

We ask this through our Lord Jesus Christ, your Son,
who lives and reigns with you and the Holy Spirit,
one God, for ever and ever.

C **Lord,**
let the Virgin Mary in her glory intercede for us;
adorned with the gifts of the Holy Spirit,
she won your favor
and brought forth for us your only Son,
fair beyond all your children on earth.
Grant that we may turn away from the ugliness of sin
and love only the beauty that comes from your Spirit.

We ask this through our Lord Jesus Christ, your Son,
who lives and reigns with you and the Holy Spirit,
one God, for ever and ever.

PRAYER OVER THE GIFTS

Lord,
grant that we may receive
the effect of the offering we dedicate to you,
so that, walking with the Blessed Virgin Mary in the way of beauty,
we may be renewed by progress in the life of the spirit
and come at last to the vision of your glory.

We ask this through Christ our Lord.

PREFACE **P 36** (Page 152)

Communion Antiphon

A **No other woman can compare with her, in the beauty of her face, in the wisdom of her words.** *See Judith 11:19-21*

B **Grace is poured forth on your lips, and so God has blessed you for ever.** *Psalm 45:3*

PRAYER AFTER COMMUNION

**Lord God,
continue to bless with your unending favor
those whom you renew in strength by this holy sacrament;
and let those to whom you have presented the Blessed Virgin Mary
in all the beauty of her virtue
walk always in the ways of your justice.**

We ask this through Christ our Lord.

37. THE BLESSED VIRGIN MARY, MOTHER OF DIVINE HOPE

The Second Vatican Council at the end of its Dogmatic Constitution on the Church *Lumen gentium* says of the Blessed Virgin that she "shines upon our world, until the day of the Lord shall come (see 2 Peter 3:10), as a sign of sure hope and comfort for your people on their pilgrim way" (no. 68). These words are found almost verbatim in the preface of the Mass of the Assumption (see *The Roman Missal* [*Sacramentary*], Pref for the Assumption, 15 August).

In considering our Lady's role in the history of salvation, the Church often refers to her as "our hope" (Final Marian Ant, *Salve, Regina,* "Hail, holy Queen"; hymn at morning prayer, 8 December, LH, 1972) and as "mother of hope" (see hymn at office of readings, 21 November, LH, 1972; see the Vulgate text of Sirach 24:24); on the birthday of our Lady the Church rejoices because she "brought the dawn of hope and salvation to the world" (PAC, 8 September); recalling her role as mother in the process of salvation, the Church sings in petition: "O gate of everlasting life,/With loving heart our prayer receive:/Through you our hope of life was born,/When hope was lost through sin of Eve" (English translation of hymn at evening prayer, 22 August, LH, 1972); in the mystery of our Lady's glorious assumption the Church looks on Mary as "the sure hope of salvation," shining on all the faithful "through life's sharp thorns" (hymn at morning prayer, 15 August, LH, 1972). On 9 July in some particular Churches there is a liturgical celebration of the Blessed Virgin Mary, Mother of Divine Hope, and notably in the Congregation of the Passion of Jesus Christ (Passionists), from whose *Proprium missarum,* Curia Generalis CP, Rome, 1974, pp. 21–22, several texts of this formulary are taken.

In this Mass the Mother of Christ is venerated:

—because in her life on earth she constantly practiced the virtue of hope; "she placed all her trust" in the Lord (Pref), "she awaited in hope and conceived in faith the Son of Man, whom the prophets had foretold" (Pref);

—because in her assumption into heaven she became the "hope of God's people" (Ent Ant); for she comes to the aid of all who have no hope (see Ent Ant) and looks with love on all who seek her help, giving them strength and comfort (see OP, A, OP, B, Ent Ant);

—because she is a "beacon of unfailing hope" and solace (OP, B) for all the children of Adam (see Pref) "until the day of the Lord dawns in glory" (Pref).

Entrance Antiphon

Hail, Virgin Mary, hope of God's people: you come to the aid of all who have no hope, you look with love on all who seek your help.

OPENING PRAYER

A **Lord our God,**
you give us the joy
of honoring the Blessed Virgin Mary
as mother of divine hope.

In your mercy
grant that, through her prayers and help,
we may always live as good citizens of this world,
with our hearts fixed on the world to come,
and so receive what we look forward to in faith,
the fulfillment of all our hope.

We ask this through our Lord Jesus Christ, your Son,
who lives and reigns with you and the Holy Spirit,
one God, for ever and ever.

B **Lord God,**
you have given the Blessed Virgin Mary to your Church
as a beacon of unfailing hope.

In your goodness
grant that those who are burdened by life's cares
may find in her consolation and strength
and that those who despair of salvation
may find their hearts warmed and uplifted
as they turn to her in their need.

We ask this through our Lord Jesus Christ, your Son,
who lives and reigns with you and the Holy Spirit,
one God, for ever and ever.

PRAYER OVER THE GIFTS

Lord,
receive with this offering
the prayers of your people,
so that, through the intercession of blessed Mary,
the mother of your Son,
no request of ours may go unanswered,
no petition may be uttered in vain.

We ask this through Christ our Lord.

PREFACE **P 37** (Page 153)

Communion Antiphon

A **Blessed are you for firmly believing that the promises of the Lord would be fulfilled.** *Luke 1:45*

B **Let us live holy and devout lives in this world as we look forward in blessed hope to the joyful coming of our great God and Savior, Jesus Christ.** *Titus 2:12-13*

PRAYER AFTER COMMUNION

Lord God,
we have received this sacrament
of faith and salvation;
as we honor the Blessed Virgin, mother of our hope,
we pray that we may come to share with her
in your own divine love.

We ask this through Christ our Lord.

38. HOLY MARY, MOTHER OF UNITY

The example of Christ as he prayed to the Father that "they all may be one" (Gos, A, John 17:21) is an encouragement to all his disciples to be earnest themselves in their prayers for Christian unity.

The Catholic Church, in its zeal for the unity of Christians, and indeed of the whole human family, asks God that, through the intercession of the Blessed Virgin, "all the families of nations . . . may be gathered together to form the one people of the New Covenant" (OP). For the Church is convinced that the cause of Christian unity rightly belongs to the spiritual motherhood of the Blessed Virgin Mary (see Leo XIII, Encyclical Letter *Adiutricem populi,* ASS 28 [1895–1896], p. 135). Hence Paul VI referred more than once to the Blessed Virgin as "mother of unity" (see *Insegnamenti di Paolo VI,* III, p. 69).

The formulary of this Mass first of all celebrates God as "fountain of unity and wellspring of harmony" (OP); then it recalls the one mediator between God and the human race, Jesus Christ (see 1 Read, 1 Timothy 2:5), who, the day before he suffered, prayed to the Father for the disciples that they might be made perfect in unity (see Gos, B, John 17:20-26); it also commemorates the Blessed Virgin, who played an important role in the history of salvation with reference to the "mystery of unity":

—*in the mystery of the incarnation,* when in her "virginal womb" the Word of God "united divine and human nature" in an unbreakable bond (POG);

—*in her virginal motherhood,* when the Son of God "chose for his mother a woman unstained in heart and body" (Pref), who would be the image of his Bride, the one and undivided Church (see Pref);

—*in the passion of Christ,* when Jesus, "lifted high above the earth, in the presence of his mother . . . gathered (God's) scattered children into unity" (Pref);

—*in the outpouring of the Holy Spirit,* when Jesus, returning to the Father, "sent upon the Blessed Virgin, at prayer with the apostles, the Spirit of concord and unity, of peace and forgiveness" (Pref; see Ent Ant, B).

Entrance Antiphon

A **Rejoice and be glad, Virgin Mary, for all God's children will be reunited and will bless the everlasting Lord.** *See Tobit 13:13*

B **With one heart the disciples continued steadfast in prayer with Mary, the mother of Jesus.** *See Acts 1:14*

OPENING PRAYER

All-holy Father,
fountain of unity and wellspring of harmony,
grant that all the families of nations,
through the intercession of the Blessed Virgin Mary,
mother of the human race,
may be gathered together
to form the one people of the New Covenant.

We make our prayer through our Lord Jesus Christ,
your Son,
who lives and reigns with you and the Holy Spirit,
one God, for ever and ever.

PRAYER OVER THE GIFTS

Lord,
as we honor the memory of the Blessed Virgin Mary,
in whose virginal womb
your Son united divine and human nature,
we earnestly beg
that this offering may become
the sacrament of our worship,
the sign of our unity,
and the bond of our love.

We ask this through Christ our Lord.

PREFACE **P 38** (Page 154)

Communion Antiphon

Because there is one bread, we, though many, are one body, for we all share in the one bread and the one cup. *See 1 Corinthians 10:17*

PRAYER AFTER COMMUNION

Lord God,
through your holy gifts
which we have received
on this memorial of holy Mary, mother of unity,
pour out upon us
the Spirit of gentleness and peace,
that we may work together in harmony
and so hasten the coming of your kingdom.

We ask this through Christ our Lord.

Section 3

This section contains eight Mass formularies for the celebration of a memorial of Mary under titles that refer to her merciful intercession on behalf of the faithful.

39. HOLY MARY, QUEEN AND MOTHER OF MERCY

The title of this formulary comprises two titles frequently attributed to the Blessed Virgin, both of which speak of her graciousness and are much loved by the faithful: "queen of mercy" and "mother of mercy."

The title "queen of mercy" (Ent Ant, OP, B, *All*) celebrates the kindness, the generosity, the dignity of the Blessed Virgin, who from her place in heaven fulfills the role of Queen Esther (see 1 Read, Esther 4:17), "never ceasing to pray" to her Son (Pref) for the salvation of her people as they confidently fly to her for refuge in their trials and dangers. The Blessed Virgin is thus the "gracious" and "compassionate" queen (Pref, PAC) "who has herself uniquely known (God's) loving kindness and stretches out her arms to embrace all who take refuge in her" (Pref; see PAC); hence she is rightly addressed as "solace of the repentant, hope of the distressed" (Ent Ant).

The title "mother of mercy" (OP, A, Pref, POG) is thought to have been first given to the Blessed Virgin by St. Odo (d. 942), Abbot of Cluny (see *Vita Odonis* I:9: PL 133:47). It is a fitting title of our Lady both because she brought forth for us Jesus Christ, the visible manifestation of the mercy of the invisible God, and because she is the spiritual mother of the faithful, full of grace and mercy; in the words of St. Lawrence of Brindisi, "the Blessed Virgin is called 'mother of mercy,' that is, the most merciful, the most compassionate mother, the most tender mother, the most loving mother" (*Mariale,* Second sermon on the "Salve Regina," III: *Opera omnia,* I, Seminary Press, Padua, 1928, p. 391). For the mother of Jesus from her place in heaven points out the needs of the faithful to her Son, with whom she interceded on earth on behalf of the bridegroom and bride of Cana (see Gos, John 2:1-11).

In this formulary the Blessed Virgin is celebrated as:

—*a prophet extolling the mercy of God* (see Gos, Luke 1:39-55): for in her Magnificat she twice praises God's mercy: "He has mercy on those who fear him in every generation"; "He has come to the help of his servant Israel, for he has remembered his promise of mercy" (Luke 1:50, 54; see Com Ant, B). The faithful therefore pray that they "may always praise (God's) mercy in company with the Blessed Virgin" (PAC);

—*a woman who has uniquely experienced God's mercy:* "She is the gracious queen who has herself uniquely known (God's) loving kindness and stretches out her arms to embrace all who . . . call upon her help in their distress" (Pref). These words of the preface echo those of Pope John Paul II: "Mary is . . . the one who obtained mercy in a particular and exceptional way, as no other person has . . . ." (Encyclical Letter *Dives in misericordia,* no. 9: AAS 72 [1980], pp. 1208–1209).

Entrance Antiphon

Hail, queen of mercy, Mother of Christ in your glory, solace of the repentant, hope of the distressed.

OPENING PRAYER

A **God, whose mercy is without measure,**
through the prayers of the Blessed Virgin Mary,
mother of mercy,
grant that we may know your loving kindness on earth
and come at last to the glory of heaven.

We make our prayer through our Lord Jesus Christ,
your Son,
who lives and reigns with you and the Holy Spirit,
one God, for ever and ever.

B **All-holy Father,**
hear the prayers of your children,
weighed down by our sinfulness,
as we turn to you and call upon the merciful love
that moved you to send your Son as Savior of the world
and to enthrone holy Mary as the queen of mercy.

We make our prayer through our Lord Jesus Christ,
your Son,
who lives and reigns with you and the Holy Spirit,
one God, for ever and ever.

PRAYER OVER THE GIFTS

Lord,
receive the gifts of your people,
and grant that as we look up
to the Blessed Virgin, mother of mercy,
we may show ourselves merciful to others
and receive your pardon toward us.

We ask this through Christ our Lord.

PREFACE **P 39** (Page 155)

Communion Antiphon

A **Be merciful as your Father is merciful.** *Luke 6:36*

B **The Almighty has done great things for me, and holy is his Name.**
He has mercy on those who fear him in every generation.
Luke 1:49-50

PRAYER AFTER COMMUNION

Lord God,
you have given us food and drink from heaven;
grant that we may always praise your mercy
in company with the Blessed Virgin
and rejoice in her protection,
for we acknowledge her as our queen,
compassionate to sinners
and merciful to the poor.

We ask this through Christ our Lord.

40. THE BLESSED VIRGIN MARY, MOTHER OF DIVINE PROVIDENCE

In 1744 Benedict XIV (d. 1758) granted to the Congregation of Clerks Regular of St. Paul (Barnabites) a Mass in honor of the Blessed Virgin Mary, "mother of divine providence," venerated at Rome in the church of St. Charles, known popularly as "ai Catinari." This Mass was to be celebrated on the Saturday before the third Sunday of November. Several other religious institutes also observe this memorial.

This title celebrates the role entrusted by God, whose "loving providence is always wise and unfailing" (OP), to the Blessed Virgin as:

—*the loving mother of Christ* (POG), for "in the wisdom of (God's) providence the Blessed Virgin Mary . . . gave birth to the Savior of the world" (Pref);
—*a mother who cares for each of her children* (Pref), "entrusted to her by Christ Jesus while he hung upon the cross" (Pref);
—*the handmaid of God's love* (see Pref), for as she interceded with her Son at Cana of Galilee for the bridegroom and the bride (see Gos, John 2:1-11; see Pref), "now, enthroned as queen at her Son's right hand, she provides for all the needs of the Church" (Pref).

The Blessed Virgin is thus called "mother of divine providence" because she has been given to us by God in his great providence as a generous mother providing us through her intercession with gifts from heaven. Like God, who cannot forget his people (see Ent Ant, Isaiah 49:15), indeed consoles them like a mother, so the Blessed Virgin has pity on us (see Ent Ant), intercedes for us (see OP, POG, PAC), comes to the help of the Church in its needs (see Pref), and fills us with consolation (see 1 Read, Isaiah 66:10-14).

Hence the faithful, relying on the patronage of so great a mother, receive "mercy and grace in (their) time of need" (POG; see Hebrews 4:16), and, as in obedience to God's command they "seek . . . above all else" God's kingdom and its justice, they "receive (God's) help for (their) earthly needs" (PAC, see Matthew 6:33).

In great part the texts of this Mass are taken from the *Missae Propriae*, Curia Generalis Clericorum Regularium sancti Pauli, Rome, 1981, pp. 60–76.

Entrance Antiphon

Can a mother forget her infant, and not have pity on the child of her womb? Even if a mother should forget, you I will never forget.

Isaiah 49:15

OPENING PRAYER

Lord our God,
your loving providence is always wise and unfailing;
through the prayers of the Blessed Virgin,
mother of your Son,
remove from us all that would harm us
and grant us all that will be for our good.

We make our prayer through our Lord Jesus Christ,
your Son,
who lives and reigns with you and the Holy Spirit,
one God, for ever and ever.

PRAYER OVER THE GIFTS

Lord,
in your goodness
accept the gifts of your Church,
so that, through the loving intercession
of the mother of your Son,
we may receive your mercy and grace
in our time of need.

We ask this through Christ our Lord.

PREFACE **P 40** (Page 156)

Communion Antiphon

Glorious things are told of you, Virgin Mary, for the Almighty has done great things for you. *See Psalm 87:3; Luke 1:49*

PRAYER AFTER COMMUNION

God of mercy,
let this heavenly table
continue to strengthen your faithful people,
so that, through the intercession of the mother of divine providence,
we may seek your kingdom and its justice
above all else
and receive your help for our earthly needs.

We ask this through Christ our Lord.

41. THE BLESSED VIRGIN MARY, MOTHER OF CONSOLATION

The actions of the all-powerful and merciful God in coming to the aid of his oppressed or exiled people are described in Scripture as "God's consolation." The supreme consolation is Christ, sent by the Father into the world when the fullness of time had come, to heal the broken-hearted (see 1 Read, Isaiah 61:1-3, 10-11).

The Blessed Virgin Mary is herself rightly named and venerated as "mother of consolation" or "comforter of the afflicted." Through her God "graciously sent Jesus Christ to be the consolation" of his people (OP).

Because she stood beside Christ suffering on the cross and endured her bitter agony, she gained in the highest degree the blessedness promised in the Gospel to those who mourn (see Gos, A, Matthew 5:5); because the Lord consoled her by the resurrection of Jesus, she in her turn is able to console her children in all their afflictions (see Ent Ant, 2 Corinthians 1:3-5).

After the ascension of Christ, "in company with the apostles she earnestly prayed and awaited with trust the coming of the Spirit of consolation and peace" (Pref, see Gos, B, John 14:15-21, 25-27).

Even now after her assumption into heaven, she continues to intercede with a mother's love for those in distress. In the Dogmatic Constitution on the Church *Lumen gentium* of the Second Vatican Council we read: "The mother of Jesus . . . shines forth as a sign of sure hope and consolation for the pilgrim people of God" (no. 68).

The Mother of the Lord is honored in many places under the title of "mother of consolation" or "comforter of the afflicted," and especially in Turin (on 20 June), where a well-known shrine is dedicated in her honor, and in a large number of religious families, and particularly in the Order of St. Augustine and the Consolata Missionary Institute (Consolata Missionaries), founded by the Servant of God Joseph Allamano (d. 1926).

Entrance Antiphon

Blessed be God, the Father of mercies and God of all comfort, who consoles us in all our afflictions. *See 2 Corinthians 1:3*

OPENING PRAYER

**Lord our God,
through the Virgin Mary
you graciously sent Jesus Christ
to be the consolation of your people;
grant that, through her intercession,
we may be filled with all consolation
and share it among our brothers and sisters.**

**We make our prayer through our Lord Jesus Christ,
your Son,
who lives and reigns with you and the Holy Spirit,
one God, for ever and ever.**

PRAYER OVER THE GIFTS

**All-holy Father,
receive this offering
from humble and joyful hearts
on this memorial of the Blessed Virgin Mary;
grant that the sacrifice of Christ in which we share
may be our consolation on earth
and our everlasting salvation.**

We ask this through Christ our Lord.

PREFACE **P 41** (Page 157)

Communion Antiphon

Glorious things are told of you, Virgin Mary; in you all rejoice to find their home. *See Psalm 87: 3, 7*

PRAYER AFTER COMMUNION

Lord God,
renewed by the sacrament of the risen Christ,
we who honor the mother of your Son
pray that, as we experience each day
the mystery of death in our bodies,
we may be uplifted by hope from heaven
and show forth in our daily lives
the Good News of the resurrection.

We ask this through Christ our Lord.

42. THE BLESSED VIRGIN MARY, HELP OF CHRISTIANS

The Church has often experienced the extraordinary help of the Mother of God in times of persecution by the enemies of the Christian faith. Therefore, from the earliest centuries of the Christian era, the custom developed of invoking the Blessed Virgin in the storms of persecution under the title of "help of Christians."

While Pius VII (d. 1823) was held a prisoner after being driven from the See of Peter by force of arms, and the whole Church was praying earnestly to God on his behalf through the intercession of the Blessed Virgin, the Supreme Pontiff was unexpectedly released and, on returning to Rome, was restored to the papal throne on 24 May 1814.

As a result Pius VII established a feast in honor of the Virgin Mother under the title of "help of Christians," to be celebrated at Rome in perpetuity on 24 May, the anniversary of his safe return to the city of Rome. This feast is celebrated in many particular Churches and religious institutes, especially in the Society of St. Francis de Sales (Salesians), founded by St. John Bosco (d. 1888).

The first reading of this Mass recalls the great conflict established by God's providence between the woman and the serpent from the beginning of the human race. There is a choice of readings:

—either Genesis 3:1-6, 13-15, recounting God's threatening words to the serpent and the first proclamation of the future victory of the Son of the woman: "I will put enmity between you and the woman, between your seed and her seed; the serpent will bruise your head, and you will strike its heel" (v. 15);

—or Revelation 12:1-3a, 7-12ab, 17, which prophetically narrates the warfare of the great dragon or ancient serpent (see vv. 3, 9) against the woman clothed with the sun and crowned with twelve stars (see v. 1), and against the rest "of her seed, who keep the commandments of God and have the witness of Jesus" (v. 17); that is, against the Church, represented under the image of the Virgin Mary.

The gospel reading (John 2:1-11) calls to mind the help that, by nourishing the faith of Christians and responding to their needs, the Blessed Virgin continuously bestows on the Church—symbolized by the disciples who believe in Jesus (see v. 11) and the guests at the wedding feast (see v. 2).

The euchological texts of the Mass celebrate the action of God in appointing the Blessed Virgin, "mother of (his) beloved Son" (OP), "mother and help of Christians" (OP, Pref), "so that under her protection we might be fearless in waging the battle of faith, steadfast in holding the teaching of the apostles, and tranquil in spirit in the storms of this world" (Pref; see OP, POG).

The texts of this Mass, except for the preface, are taken, with some changes, from the *Propria missarum* of the Society of St. Francis de Sales (Vatican Polyglot Press, 1974, pp. 35–40) and that of the Congregation of Clerks Regular of St. Paul (Curia Generalis, Rome, 1981, pp. 25–29).

Entrance Antiphon

People will never cease to praise you, as they recall the power of the Lord for ever. *See Judith 13:19*

OPENING PRAYER

Lord our God,
you chose the mother of your beloved Son
to be the mother and help of Christians;
grant that we may live under her protection
and that your Church may enjoy unbroken peace.

We make our prayer through our Lord Jesus Christ,
your Son,
who lives and reigns with you and the Holy Spirit,
one God, for ever and ever.

PRAYER OVER THE GIFTS

Lord,
we offer you this sacrifice of praise
as we rejoice in this memorial of the mother of your Son;
grant that through the help of so great a mother
we may find you coming to our rescue in every trial.

We ask this through Christ our Lord.

PREFACE **P 42** (Page 158)

Communion Antiphon

The Lord, who has done great things for you, is your praise and your God. *Deuteronomy 10:21a*

PRAYER AFTER COMMUNION

**Lord God,
refreshed by this heavenly sacrament
and relying on the help of the Blessed Virgin Mary,
we ask that we may cast aside the old ways of sin
and put on Jesus Christ,
the author of the new creation,
who lives and reigns for ever and ever.**

43. OUR LADY OF RANSOM

Among the religious families dedicated by a special bond to the Mother of Christ is the Order of Our Lady of Ransom, founded for the ransom of Christian captives by St. Peter Nolasco (d. 1256) in Barcelona in 1218, after consultation with St. Raymond of Penyafort (d. 1275) and King James I of Aragon (d. 1276).

Our Lady of Ransom is especially venerated in Aragon and Catalonia and in many regions of Latin America.

This formulary, in view of the purpose for which the Order (the Mercedarians) was founded, is primarily a celebration of Christ as ''Redeemer of the human race'' (OP), who merited by his sacrifice ''the true liberty of (God's) children'' (OP).

It is also a commemoration of our Lady, who is rightly called ''the handmaid of our redemption'' (Pref) because she is the handmaid of the Lord (see Luke 1:38), totally dedicated to the work of her Son, the Redeemer (see LG, no. 56).

In this Mass our Lady is celebrated as:

—*a new Judith:* just as the first Judith courageously freed her people from the siege by Holofernes, so Mary in her warfare against the serpent, the ancient enemy, brought blessings on the people of Israel and on the whole Church (see 1 Read, Judith 15:8-10; 16:13-14);
—*the prophetess of the redemption of Israel:* becoming the voice of her people, she magnified the Lord, because, mindful of his mercy, he had come to the rescue of Israel by redeeming it from slavery to sin (see Ent Ant, Luke 1:46a, 54-55a);
—*the companion in the passion of Christ:* our Lady was a loving mother of her Son ''in his infancy'' and stood at the foot of his cross ''as the faithful companion in his passion'' (Pref); the gospel reading is appropriately taken from the passage in John recording her presence beside the cross (Gos, John 19:25-27);
—*a loving mother,* given to us by God in his mercy (see PAC), one who ''cares unceasingly with a mother's love for all (God's) children in their need, breaking the chains of every form of captivity, that (we) might enjoy full liberty of body and spirit'' (Pref);
—''*our advocate*'' (Pref) and ''*patroness in heaven*'' (PAC): Mary, ''assumed into heaven'' (Pref), is always interceding for us.

The texts of this Mass are taken from the *Proprium missarum Ordinis beatae Mariae Virginis de Mercede,* Curia Generalis Ordinis, Rome, 1976, pp. 26–28 and 50.

Entrance Antiphon

My soul proclaims the greatness of the Lord. He has come to the help of his servant Israel, for he has remembered his promise of mercy, the promise made to our ancestors. *Luke 1:46a, 54-55a*

OPENING PRAYER

God, the Father of mercies,
you sent your Son into the world
as Redeemer of the human race;
grant that we who honor his mother as Our Lady of Ransom
may faithfully protect
and seek to spread to all peoples
the true liberty of your children,
which Christ the Lord merited by his sacrifice.

We ask this through our Lord Jesus Christ, your Son,
who lives and reigns with you and the Holy Spirit,
one God, for ever and ever.

PRAYER OVER THE GIFTS

Lord,
accept the gifts we offer in worship;
and grant that we who celebrate this memorial
of the boundless love of your Son
may be strengthened
by the example of the Blessed Virgin Mary
in our love for you and for our neighbor.

We ask this through Christ our Lord.

PREFACE **P 43** (Page 159)

Communion Antiphon

The mother of Jesus said to the attendants: Do whatever he tells you.
John 2:5

PRAYER AFTER COMMUNION

**Lord God,
we have received the sacrament of redemption and life
and now pray that through the intercession of Our Lady of Ransom,
whom in your mercy you gave us
as our loving mother and patroness in heaven,
we may serve ever more strenuously
the mystery of salvation on earth
and be at last admitted into your heavenly kingdom.**

We ask this through Christ our Lord.

44. THE BLESSED VIRGIN MARY, HEALTH OF THE SICK

Divine healing affects our whole human nature, body, soul, and spirit, while we are pilgrims here on earth and especially citizens of heaven. Through the healing made possible by Christ in the Holy Spirit, our human condition is completely altered: oppression is changed into liberty, ignorance into knowledge of the truth, sickness into health, affliction into joy, death into life, slavery to sin into a share in the divine nature. Yet we cannot achieve absolute and perfect healing in this world: our life is exposed to suffering, illness, and death. But ''God's healing'' is Jesus Christ himself, whom the Father sent into the world as our Savior and as the physician of body and soul, as the liturgy describes him, echoing the words of St. Ignatius of Antioch (see *Ad Ephesios,* VII, 2: Sch, 10, p. 74). In the days of his flesh, moved by compassion, he healed many sick people, often freeing them at the same time from the wound of sin.

Our Lady also, as the mother of Christ, our Savior, and mother of the faithful, with heartfelt love comes to the help of her children in their troubles. That is why sick people flock to her in great numbers, often going to shrines dedicated to her, so that they may be healed through her intercession. In these Marian shrines there are many testimonies to the confidence that sick people have in the mother of Christ.

Among the titles under which the Blessed Virgin is venerated by the sick that of ''health of the sick'' is preeminent. It was made popular especially through the zeal of the members of the Order of Clerks Regular, Ministers to the Sick, whose church of St. Mary Magdalene in Rome possesses a Marian image celebrated for its veneration by the faithful and the miracles associated with it.

In the liturgy of the word one of Isaiah's Songs of the Servant is read (1 Read, Isaiah 53:1-5, 7-10): ''he has borne our griefs and carried our sorrows'' (v. 4), ''with his stripes we are healed'' (v. 5). The congregation responds by blessing God, ''who heals all . . . ills'' (Resp, Psalm 103:1a, 3b).

The gospel reading is from St. Luke's account of the visitation (Gos, Luke 1:39-56), so that the faithful, as they see our Lady, full of faith and praising God's loving kindness, hastening to visit the mother of the Precursor, may be inspired to show the same loving care to their sick brothers and sisters.

In the liturgy of the eucharist God the Father is glorified for giving to the sick a patroness and model in our Lady:

—*a patroness,* because to the sick who call on her patronage ''she now shines radiantly as a sign of health, of healing, and of divine hope'' (Pref);
—*a model,* because ''to all who look up to her in prayer'' she is ''the model of perfect acceptance of (God's) will and of wholehearted conformity with Christ'' (Pref).

To arrange Masses in honor of our Lady, health of the sick, and to ask her intercession for the recovery of health is to celebrate the unique importance of the history of salvation, which will be brought to its completion and perfection when, in the coming of Christ in glory, ''the last enemy to be destroyed will be death'' (1 Corinthians 15:26), and the bodies of the just will rise in incorruption.

The texts of this Mass, except for the preface, are those to be found in the Mass of the Blessed Virgin Mary, Health of the Sick, from the *Proprium missarum Ordinis Ministrantium infirmis,* Vatican Polyglot Press, 1974, pp. 14–15, 27-30.

Entrance Antiphon

I am the Savior of my people. Whatever their troubles I will answer their cry. *See Psalm 35:3; Jonah 2:3*

OPENING PRAYER

Lord our God,
in answer to the prayers
of the blessed and ever virgin Mary in her glory,
grant to us, your servants,
unfailing health in body and in mind,
freedom from sorrow in this life,
and everlasting joy in heaven.

We ask this through our Lord Jesus Christ, your Son,
who lives and reigns with you and the Holy Spirit,
one God, for ever and ever.

PRAYER OVER THE GIFTS

Lord,
on this memorial of blessed Mary, Mother of God,
look with favor on the prayers and offerings
presented by your faithful people.

Grant that these offerings may be acceptable to you
and so bring us the help of your loving compassion.

We ask this through Christ our Lord.

PREFACE **P 44** (Page 160)

Communion Antiphon

The Lord, my strength and my song, has become my Savior.

Psalm 118:14

PRAYER AFTER COMMUNION

Lord our God,
on this memorial of the Blessed Virgin Mary, the mother of Jesus,
we have received with joyful hearts
the healing sacrament
of the body and blood of your only Son;
may this sacrament bring us blessings in this life
and in the world to come.

We ask this through Christ our Lord.

45. THE BLESSED VIRGIN MARY, QUEEN OF PEACE

Because of her close personal connection with her Son, the "Prince of Peace" (Ent Ant, Isaiah 9:6; 1 Read, Isaiah 9:1- 3, 5-6), our Lady has been increasingly venerated as "queen of peace": in the calendars of particular Churches and some religious institutes there is a memorial of her as "queen of peace." It is worth recalling that Benedict XV in 1917, while a terrible war was raging, ordered that the invocation "queen of peace" should be added to the Litany of Loreto.

This Mass commemorates the cooperation of our Lady in the reconciliation or "peace" between God and the human family brought about by Christ:

—*in the mystery of the incarnation:* the lowly handmaid of the Lord receives God's word from the angel Gabriel and conceives in her virginal womb the Prince of Peace (see Pref; see Gos, Luke 1:26-38), who "has restored our peace, reconciling in himself earth with heaven" (Com Ant);

—*in the mystery of the passion:* the faithful mother stands "fearless beside the cross as her Son sheds his blood for our salvation and reconciles all things to himself in peace" (Pref);

—*in the mystery of Pentecost:* our Lady, the daughter of peace, joins "in prayer with the apostles as she awaits . . . the Spirit of unity and peace, of love and joy" (Pref).

In celebrating the memorial of the Blessed Virgin Mary, Queen of Peace, the assembly of the faithful begs God that through her intercession he will grant to the Church and to the human family these favors:

—*the spirit of love:* "that we may live in peace as one family, united in love for one another" (OP); "fill us with the spirit of love" (PAC);

—*the gifts of unity and peace:* "bestows on your family the gifts of unity and peace" (POG); "that we may live in peace as one family" (OP); that "we may build up in our world the peace that Christ left with us" (PAC);

—*tranquility in our times:* "hear our earnest prayer: grant that our times may be tranquil" (OP).

The texts of this Mass, except for the preface, are taken from the booklet *Proprio delle messe per le diocesi di Savona e Noli,* Tipografia Priamar, Savona, 1978, p. 17.

Entrance Antiphon

A child is born for us, a son is given to us, and he shall be called "Prince of Peace." *See Isaiah 9:6*

OPENING PRAYER

Lord our God,
you sent your only Son
to bring peace to our world.

Through the intercession
of Blessed Mary, ever virgin,
hear our earnest prayer;
grant that our times may be tranquil,
so that we may live in peace as one family,
united in love for one another.

We ask this through our Lord Jesus Christ, your Son,
who lives and reigns with you and the Holy Spirit,
one God, for ever and ever.

PRAYER OVER THE GIFTS

Lord,
as we lovingly venerate
Blessed Mary, ever virgin, as queen of peace,
we offer you the sacrifice of reconciliation;
be pleased with our offering
and bestow on your family
the gifts of unity and peace.

We ask this through Christ our Lord.

PREFACE **P 45** (Page 161)

Communion Antiphon

A virgin has given birth to one who is truly God and truly human: God has restored our peace, reconciling in himself earth with heaven.

PRAYER AFTER COMMUNION

Lord our God,
on this memorial of our Lady, queen of peace,
fill us with the spirit of love,
so that, refreshed by the body and blood of your only Son,
we may build up in our world
the peace that Christ left with us.

We ask this through Christ our Lord.

46. THE BLESSED VIRGIN MARY, GATE OF HEAVEN

The final formulary in this collection of Masses of the Blessed Virgin Mary celebrates the Mother of God as she lovingly accompanies God's people on their pilgrimage to their true home in heaven.

The eschatological sense proper to the celebration of the eucharist is central to this Mass: the assembly of the faithful contemplates ''the holy city, the new Jerusalem, . . . arrayed like a bride for her husband,'' and hears the voice of the Lord from the heavenly throne, saying: ''See, I make all things new'' (see 1 Read, Revelation 21:1-5a). This future state of the Church has already been realized in our Lady, virgin and bride, in all her beauty, without stain or wrinkle (see Ephesians 5:27). The faithful joyfully go up ''to the house of the Lord,'' where they will praise his name for ever (see Resp, Psalm 122:1-2, 3-4, 8-9). They are to stay watchful in order to go out to meet the Bridegroom with lighted lamps, so that when the door is opened they may be worthy of admission (see Gos, Matthew 25:1-13).

This Mass primarily celebrates Christ the Lord, whom his loving Father has made ''the gateway to salvation and life'' (OP; see John 10:7): Jesus, ''who . . . opens the door of forgiveness'' (Pref), through whom the gate of God's city in heaven has been thrown open to us (see OP).

The metaphors of ''door'' or ''entrance'' or ''gate'' or ''threshold'' have been applied from patristic times to our Lady to express her function as the second Eve, to express her virginal motherhood or her intercession for the faithful.

In this formulary our Lady is celebrated as:

—*the sinless Eve,* who has overcome the pride of the first woman by humility, Eve's disbelief by faith, reopening what had been closed: ''She is the humble Virgin, whose faith opened the gate of eternal life, closed by the disbelief of Eve'' (Pref); ''the gates of paradise, closed by Eve, were reopened by you, O Virgin Mary'' *(All);*

—*the Virgin Mother of Christ:* through her motherhood Mary is ''the very gate of life,'' because from her ''the Savior of the world came among us, Jesus Christ our Lord'' (POG); the ''resplendent gate of light,'' through whom ''there came to shine on us Christ, the light of the world'' (Com Ant); the ''Maiden-Mother, bearing the Word of God, . . . the gate of paradise,'' who ''in bringing God into the world'' has ''unlocked for us the gate of heaven'' (Ent Ant);

—*the prayerful voice of intercession* (see Pref): the Church does not doubt that ''through the Blessed Virgin Mary, who brought our Savior into the world, (God's) gifts of grace may come down on us and the gate of heaven may be opened to receive us into the joy of (God's) kingdom'' (PAC).

Entrance Antiphon

Maiden-Mother, bearing the Word of God, you are the gate of paradise; in bringing God into the world you have unlocked for us the gate of heaven.

OPENING PRAYER

**Lord our God,
in your goodness
you have made your Son
the gateway to salvation and life;
grant that, as we follow the example
of the Blessed Virgin Mary,
we may remain faithful in the love of Christ
and so pass safely through the gate
of your city in heaven.**

**We ask this through our Lord Jesus Christ, your Son,
who lives and reigns with you and the Holy Spirit,
one God, for ever and ever.**

PRAYER OVER THE GIFTS

**Lord,
we offer to the glory of your name
the sacrament of unity and peace
as we honor the memory of the glorious Virgin Mary,
the very gate of life,
through whom the Savior of the world came among us,
Jesus Christ our Lord,
who lives and reigns for ever and ever.**

PREFACE **P 46** (Page 162)

Communion Antiphon

Blessed are you, Virgin Mary, resplendent gate of light; through you there came to shine on us Christ, the light of the world.

PRAYER AFTER COMMUNION

Refreshed, Lord God, by this joyous sacrament,
we pray that through the Blessed Virgin Mary,
who brought our Savior into the world,
your gifts of grace may come down on us
and the gate of heaven may be opened to receive us
into the joy of your kingdom.

We ask this through Christ our Lord.

ALPHABETICAL INDEX OF MASSES

ALPHABETICAL INDEX OF PREFACES